LOUIS KAHN

LOUIS

CARTER WISEMAN

KAHN

A LIFE IN ARCHITECTURE

UNIVERSITY OF VIRGINIA PRESS | *Charlottesville and London*

University of Virginia Press

Printed in the United States of America on acid-free paper

First published 2020

9 8 7 6 5 4 3 2 1

ISBN 978-0-8139-4497-5 (paper)
ISBN 978-0-8139-4750-1 (ebook)

Library of Congress Cataloging-in-Publication Data is available for this title.

Cover photographs: Lionel Freedman, gelatin silver print, "Louis Kahn looking at his tetrahedral ceiling in the Yale University Art Gallery," 1953. (*front*; © Lionel Freedman Archives [https://lionelfreedmanarchives.com], Courtesy of Maya Myers/Yale University Art Gallery); Franklin D. Roosevelt Four Freedoms Park, Roosevelt Island, New York City (*back*; © 2012 Paul Warchol [https://warcholphotography.com/])

To my family, and my students

CONTENTS

LOUIS KAHN

INTRODUCTION

In a review of a retrospective exhibition of Louis I. Kahn's career in 2016, a leading American architecture critic referred to the "shadow his work continues to cast" on the architectural profession.[1] The choice of words was apt. Kahn's legacy involves more than conventional influence or impact, and it is devilishly difficult to analyze. Few architects have had the aesthetic courage to imitate Kahn's work, and none of those who did have matched their source of inspiration. Buildings designed by many of Kahn's contemporaries can be almost instantly dated through their forms or materials. Ludwig Mies van der Rohe's glass-and-steel Seagram Building in New York City (1958) is an icon of its day. Paul Rudolph's bush-hammered concrete Art and Architecture Building at Yale University is instantly recognizable as a work of the early 1960s. Robert Venturi's historicist house for his mother is unmistakably 1964. I. M. Pei's imposing East Building of the National Gallery (1978) is equally a creation of its time. Kahn's buildings are not so easy to place in the chronology of modernism. There are many reasons for this, but the main one is that they are products of a creative imagination informed not only by academic training and deep historical understanding, but also by an immeasurable aesthetic intuition.

The shadowy nature of Kahn's legacy is compounded by his famously cryptic pronouncements, which were recorded by students and followers who were sometimes unsure themselves of what the architect meant when he uttered them. Take his declaration, "The structure of the room must be evident in the room itself. Structure, I believe, is the giver of light."[2] The

FIGURE 1. Louis I. Kahn on the construction site of the Yale Center for British Art. (Manuscripts and Archives, Yale University Library)

claim, like so many others Kahn made, is open to endless interpretation, but a surprising number of Kahn followers will insist that they alone understand what he meant.

Another obstacle to a thorough understanding of Kahn's work is his unusual adult biography. He was married to the same woman for forty-four years, but he had several extramarital relationships, two of which produced children. The happily married wife of one of Kahn's clients declared in her husband's presence that Kahn—despite his short stature (he was 5′ 6″), the thick glasses he wore late in life, and facial scars—was "the sexiest man I ever met."[3] Kahn had an equally magnetic effect on many men, several of whom labored in his office for years in substandard conditions and for low pay but continued to revere him long after his death. One collaborator was certain that Kahn was the reincarnation of an ancient Indian holy man. This is heady stuff, and hard for any writer about Kahn to resist. But concentrating on Kahn's personal history can cloud the merits of his work. Speaking for many observers of Kahn's career, one critic noted that "the turmoil of his life came to overshadow his accomplishments."[4]

As time passes, however, one has to wonder how relevant the personal lives of great artists are to their art. While early experiences may make lasting marks on any individual, linking an artist's mature life and work carries high risks of misinterpretation, and is probably best left in the realm of speculation.

We have long known that Frank Lloyd Wright was an unfaithful husband and failed to pay his debts. But can we connect that to the horizontality of his Prairie-style buildings? More recently we have learned that Le Corbusier, one of the pioneers of architectural modernism, eagerly associated with the Vichy regime in France, something for which many people were executed.[5] Does Le Corbusier's coziness with fascists tell us anything about the way he used light in the chapel at Ronchamp, which Kahn so admired? Ludwig Mies van der Rohe, who came to the United States in 1938, allowed many supporters to think that he was a political refugee from the Nazis. But recent scholarship informs us that Mies would happily have worked for the Nazis if his flat-roofed aesthetic had not conflicted with their "volkish" fondness for gables and masonry.[6]

One might say that Kahn, because he was at once charismatic and given to mystical-sounding pronouncements, inadvertently allowed his supporters to make of him a vessel for their interpretations. While it is reasonable to wonder if his physical homeliness drove his pursuit of beautiful women, it is harder to locate any mark of such personal insecurity in the shaping of his buildings. At least one former colleague of Kahn's has suggested that there was a relationship between Kahn's facial scars and his desire to leave imperfections in his buildings. The suggestion is intriguing, but it cannot be documented, and therefore tends to obscure an appreciation of the work.

A more productive measure of Kahn's impact is the care with which the owners of his buildings have looked after them. Not all of their efforts have been successful. The government center in Bangladesh has suffered from physical deterioration and the effects of political turmoil. The impoverished nation has not been able to maintain its monument as it might have liked, and concerns about security have forced the government to ban visitors from the public spaces that were central to Kahn's original democratic concept. Nevertheless, the Bangladeshis continue to revere the building, and conservation efforts have begun. An image of it remains on their currency. In India, the Institute of Management that Kahn designed for the city of Ahmedabad has been expanded to mixed reviews, while the original buildings were damaged by an earthquake in 2001 and have since been subject to insensitive upkeep. Indeed, Kahn had personally trained local bricklayers how to lay their mortar to create subtle shadows, but some years ago the walls were given a coat of red paint, obscuring the architect's delicate intent. At least plans to demolish Kahn's main buildings have been abandoned, and a renovation campaign is in the planning stages.

The story has been happier in the United States. Kahn's addition to the Yale University Art Gallery has been restored to its original condition. His Trenton Bath House in New Jersey has been preserved, and the Alfred Newton Richards Medical Research Building at the University of Pennsylvania is under restoration. The Salk Institute for Biological Studies in La Jolla, California, perhaps Kahn's most iconic creation, has also been renovated according to the original design. A plan to add to the Kimbell Art Museum in Fort Worth, Texas—by essentially cloning the original vault-like forms—was defeated with the help of protests by members of the Kahn family and an international consortium of architects and historians. The museum eventually commissioned a nearby addition, designed by Renzo Piano, which is deferential to the original, even though it compromises the original approach to the museum.

Phillips Exeter Academy in New Hampshire committed $40 million to rectify the failures in the weatherproofing of Kahn's library there, but only after defeating an effort by some alumni to demolish the building and replace it with something more efficient. The library is now considered the jewel of the campus and receives legions of visitors more interested in Kahn's architecture than the school that commissioned it.

Surely the strongest example of how the users have come to appreciate Kahn's work is the Yale Center for British Art. By 2010, the YCBA was in need of repairs that any building of its age requires. But routine renovation was out of the question. Instead, Yale closed the building for sixteen months and invested $33 million to maintain the spirit of the original, down to the new linen wall coverings and the natural-wool carpets. A few changes were made in the allocation of space, but every effort was made to preserve what had come to be appreciated as the most important work of art in the collection: the gallery itself.

This book is an attempt to document and provide context for the most prominent and enduring of Louis Kahn's built works and the circumstances of their creation. It makes only a limited attempt to explain the sources of what many chroniclers of his work can only call genius. Doing that properly must be done by each of us alone.

ONE | THE BIRTH OF A VISION

Although not as well known as many of his contemporaries, Louis I. Kahn is considered by many in the architectural world to be on an artistic level with the most prominent practitioners of twentieth-century design—Frank Lloyd Wright, Le Corbusier, and Ludwig Mies van der Rohe, to name only the most familiar figures. Yet different as these masters were from one another in national origin (American, Swiss-French, German, respectively), all had some formative social similarities in common. Wright was born into a sturdy Wisconsin family of independent ways and high aspirations; his father was a clergyman and his mother a teacher. Le Corbusier (originally named Charles-Edouard Jeanneret-Gris) grew up in relative comfort in the Swiss city of La Chaux-de-Fonds with a father who was a watchmaker: his mother taught piano. Mies's family were stonemasons who specialized in mantel pieces and tombstones in the wealthy German city of Aachen, once the capital of Charlemagne's empire. None of these masters-to-be was wealthy at birth, but all were raised in stable communities that provided professional encouragement and opportunity.

The architects who had formed American architecture in the era preceding Kahn's were no less fortunate. Charles Follen McKim, Ralph Adams Cram, Bertram Grosvenor Goodhue, Richard Morris Hunt, and most of the other leading talents of the late nineteenth and early twentieth centuries were also blessed with economic and social good fortune. So were the men (Theodate Pope Riddle was among the few prominent women architects at the time) who would shape American architecture as members of Kahn's own generation, among them Edward Durell Stone (b. 1902), Philip Johnson (b. 1906), and Eero Saarinen (b. 1910). Most of these architects had the additional advantage of growing up in circumstances that would advance their careers. As the architectural historian Roxanne Kuter Williamson has pointed out, aspiring architects in the United States during this period almost always benefited from "family advantage, schools, and social connections." She notes that "it would be naïve to overlook the fact that, in most careers, an avid contender for fame or financial success often gains considerable advantage from a social background providing natural contact with power brokers. For architects, this means contact with wealthy potential clients and with decision-makers, whether they are politically or socially based."[1] Even in Kahn's day, the members of what was essentially a fraternity of homogeneous professionals could look forward to careers largely dependent on referrals and commissions from people very much like themselves. Few of these architects were religiously observant, but apart from such exceptions as Ely Jacques Kahn, Max Abramovitz, and Gordon Bunshaft, they were all Christians.

Kahn's circumstances were radically different. While it is dangerous to ascribe too much influence to an artist's birth and youthful experience, it is fair to suggest that Kahn's origins had at least some impact on his later work and distinguished it from that of his peers in dramatic and subtle ways.

A hefty shelf of books on Kahn has made the details of his early life familiar. The child who became Louis Isadore Kahn could not have been born much further from privilege or lower on the ladder to greatness. The parents of Leiser-Itze Schmulowsky, as Kahn was known at his birth on March 5 (or February 20 by the Julian calendar then in use) in 1901 were Estonian Jews. Some doubt lingers about precisely where they were living when their first child was born, but it was either in Parnu, on the Estonian mainland, or on the island of Osel, today called Saaremaa, off Estonia's west coast in the Baltic Sea. In any case, the boy spent his early years on Saaremaa, the largest of the Estonian islands. It is known now, as it was then, for its beers, windmills, and a well-preserved fourteenth-century castle (see color plate 1) whose austere and durable masonry forms may have imprinted even a very young boy susceptible to architecture. At the time, Estonia was part of the Russian empire. Leiser-Itze's father, Leopold, had served as a paymaster in the Russian army, but when he returned to civilian life he worked as a craftsman in stained glass. His Latvian-born—and German-speaking—wife, Bertha Mendelsohn, although from comparably humble origins, played the harp, read Goethe and Schiller, and entertained herself and the family by singing songs by Franz Schubert.

Civilized as Leiser-Itze's surroundings were for a relatively poor child, at one point they proved nearly fatal. According to family lore, the Saaremaa house was heated by a coal fire. At the age of three, Leiser-Itze was playing near the open grate. Years later, he remembered being drawn to the unusual green color of the flames, which were normally blue but could change unexpectedly. He recalled reaching toward the glowing coals, which set his clothes on fire. He covered his eyes, but the flames burned his lower face badly before his mother could put them out. Kahn barely survived, and the resulting scars around his cheeks and mouth would be permanent.

Although other members of the family had already left Estonia for the United States before Leiser-Itze's birth—some perhaps to escape Russia's anti-Semitism, some to improve their economic opportunities—Leopold's reason to follow may have been based on concerns that he might be recalled to the Russian army to fight in the expected war with Japan. War indeed broke out in 1905, but by then Leopold had left for America. Arriving in Philadelphia, where he made contact with the relatives who had preceded him, he was hoping that a half brother who ran a shop in the city might help him get started. Bertha, Leizer-Itze, his younger sister Sara, and their brother, Oscar, followed him a year later.

The family settled in a section of Philadelphia known as the Northern Liberties, named for its location outside the boundaries of William Penn's original seventeenth-century plan for the city. Although anti-Semitism in the United States in 1906 was not as pronounced as the much more oppressive conditions in Estonia, it was present nonetheless. Like most older American cities, Philadelphia was divided by ethnicity, race, and economic class. The so-called Proper Philadelphians, descendants of the early colonists, occupied the highest social strata, and gradually dispersed along the "Main Line," created by the extension of rail service to the western suburbs. More recent arrivals were consigned to lesser locations. Even the immigrant population had its system of stratification: most of the Jewish arrivals from Eastern Europe were clustered in distinct areas of the city, largely shunned even by the Jews of German origin, whose roots ran deeper in Philadelphia and who considered themselves socially superior to the newcomers. Perhaps in response to this, when the family in 1915 applied for citizenship, their name was changed to Kahn, which was certainly easier for English-speakers to spell, but might also have been considered more German-sounding. Leiser-Itze became Louis Isadore.

Family members recall that during this period the Kahns lived in a succession of two- and three-story row houses and moved frequently because they often could not pay the rent; the family had some seventeen homes in the space of two years.

At the time, the Northern Liberties was a teeming area clogged by the pushcarts that characterized many Jewish enclaves in American cities. In 1890, there were fewer than 10,000 eastern European Jews in Philadelphia; in 1910, the Russian Jewish population, which would have included the Kahns, exceeded 100,000. Because of the heat during the summer, Louis and his friends spent much of their time playing on the streets, an exposure to urban socialization that may have contributed to Kahn's later sensitivity to the way people interacted in and around his buildings.

FIGURE 2. Philadelphia's Independence Hall, around 1904, the year Kahn arrived in the United States. (The Picture Art Collection/Alamy Stock Photo)

As it turned out, Leopold's half brother was of little help to his newly arrived relative, so Leopold tried his hand at a variety of jobs, including one at a candy store, but eventually accepted what must have been a humiliating position for a skilled craftsman: a laborer building roads. Within two years, Leopold had injured his back, and he never had full-time work again, forcing his wife to assume the support of the family. Bertha found work knitting coats and blankets for a local textile company, and managed to cover costs, but the family was far from prosperous.

Despite their relative poverty, the Kahns managed, but Louis faced further difficulties. He contracted scarlet fever and was confined to a local hospital. Although he recovered, the disease left him with an unusually high-pitched voice, which would remain with him throughout his life. His hospital stay also delayed his formal schooling until the age of seven. His late start, combined with the odd speaking voice and the scars left from the accident in Estonia, no doubt had an impact on Louis's relationships with his contemporaries. His wife, Esther, recalled many years later that as a boy he was sufficiently sensitive about his appearance that he would use back alleys to walk to school so he could avoid being teased by local bullies. Kahn told his daughter Alexandra when she was young that his classmates had mocked him with taunts of "scarface."[2]

Whatever Louis's feelings about his disadvantages, they were soon compensated for by his success in school. The Philadelphia in which Louis grew up, with its Quaker roots, had a powerful tradition of high-quality public education and a commitment to helping the disadvantaged. Even in his early school years, Louis was a precocious student, and was apparently well liked by his teachers, including a Miss Apple, whom he remembered years later for her early encouragement.[3] He showed a natural talent for drawing, and Kahn's son, Nathaniel, recalled hearing that because the family could not afford pencils, they gave Louis sticks of charcoal, which he used to produce drawings that he then sold to ease the family's financial load.[4] At school, Louis's teachers quickly recognized his gifts and encouraged him to pursue them at the Public Industrial Art School. The school's director, J. Liberty Tadd, was a dedicated Quaker who supported the development of talent, especially among the poor.

Tadd—who had studied with the renowned painter, sculptor, and photographer Thomas Eakins—was a strong advocate of the Progressive movement, which held that education was an organic process, and that each student should be considered a unique individual whose learning would be tailored accordingly. Tadd described the role of the teacher as recognizing that "each mind or soul is an immortal part of the future heaven he or she is helping to build."[5] One of Tadd's exercises was to teach students how to draw with either hand, a skill that would pay professional dividends for Kahn years later when he demonstrated it to his own students. Tadd was so impressed with Louis's work that he moved him on to Philadelphia's

Central High School. On the side, the industrious Louis took art classes at the Graphic Sketch Club, later the Fleisher Art Memorial, whose founder, Samuel S. Fleisher, had declared in its 1898 mission statement that it should invite "the world to come and learn art."

Although Louis never had any formal instruction on an instrument, and had never learned to read a score, he showed an early talent for music. According to Kahn's wife, Louis's family at one point shared a house with a woman who was eager to give their daughter piano lessons. She managed to buy a piano, and Louis was allowed to sit in on the lessons. He proved so adept that he picked up the skill by ear, and was soon proficient enough to accompany silent films for pay in the local movie theaters.

While music remained important to Louis's life, his drafting skills proved stronger, winning him a four-year merit scholarship to the Pennsylvania Academy of the Fine Arts, one of the premier art schools in the country; he seemed destined for a future as a painter. But in his final year in high school, he took a course with a teacher named William F. Gray. Kahn later remembered Gray as a tall, imposing figure with "a blond-gray goatee" who called on his experience as a former architectural critic to introduce his students to the enduring monuments of ancient Egypt, Greece, and Rome, as well as the cathedrals of the Gothic period and the palaces of the Renaissance.

Gray's architectural history course evidently made an indelible mark. As Kahn remembered Gray's lectures many years later—in what had become a characteristically free-form way of speaking—they "just made my almost . . . well . . . my desire, my really strong desire to be a painter fade. Architecture struck me between the eye and the eyeball, let's put it that way." What appealed to him, he said, was that architecture was an art "you can walk around and be in. And life-size."[6] On the strength of that revelation, Kahn decided to give up the academy scholarship and in 1920 entered the architecture program at the University of Pennsylvania.

At the time, virtually all advanced academic training in architecture in the United States was based on the system developed over decades at the Ecole des Beaux-Arts in Paris. The program was painfully rigorous, requiring students to spend up to four years studying, measuring, and drawing classical monuments and distilling their principles into precisely rendered designs in ink and colored wash, which would prepare them for service to the French establishment. At the core of the program was a concentration on symmetry, imposing forms, and classically inspired details. Among the definitive examples of work at the Ecole that Kahn would have studied were Henri Labrouste's Bibliotheque Ste-Genevieve (1850) and Charles Garnier's Palais Garnier (1875), both in Paris.

For most aspiring American architects, however, training in the profession came through apprenticeship in the office of an established professional. Stanford White learned his trade in the office of Henry Hobson Richardson, and Frank Lloyd Wright worked for Louis Sullivan. But a course of study at the Ecole meant enhanced and enduring credibility at home. The first American to earn a diploma there was Richard Morris Hunt, who went on to design the sprawling Biltmore estate (1895) in Asheville, North Carolina, for the Vanderbilt family. Hunt was followed to Paris by a growing number of Americans in search of advanced training, many of them graduates of the University of Pennsylvania. The first American architecture school was founded at the Massachusetts Institute of Technology (MIT) in 1865, followed by Columbia in 1881. Penn launched its architecture program in 1890, which by 1920 was widely considered the finest in the country. Part of the reason was its star faculty member, Paul Philippe Cret.

Born in France in 1876, Cret was a 1903 graduate of the Ecole who had been persuaded to move to America by Penn alumni who had studied with him in Paris. Drawing on his experience in France, Cret developed a program in Philadelphia devoted to "the planning of important city improvements, the planning of government buildings and important memorial

FIGURE 3. The main courtyard of the University of Pennsylvania, designed by Cope and Stewardson (1895). (University Archives and Records Center, University of Pennsylvania)

buildings."[7] The teaching was carried out along Beaux-Arts lines in ateliers, or small groups of students working with one distinguished professor. The catalog of the school when Kahn attended emphasized that "the course of study is organized upon the principle that architecture is primarily a fine art."[8] Accordingly, in addition to instruction in mathematics, heating and ventilation, and concrete construction, students were required to take courses in the history of ancient and medieval architecture, the history of ornament, and watercolor rendering. Kahn had to pay his way through Penn, and his drafting skills allowed him to charge his classmates for assisting with their presentation drawings. That income, as well as money from a teaching assistantship and some borrowing, got him through.

During World War One, Cret returned to France and served as an interpreter with the American Army's First Division under General John Pershing, receiving the Croix de Guerre on his discharge in 1919. When Cret

FIGURE 4. The University of Pennsylvania library (1891), designed by Frank Furness, where Kahn taught his Master Class. (Detroit Publishing Company Collection, Library of Congress, Prints and Photographs Division)

returned to Penn, he embarked on a number of civic projects; among the most distinguished were the Detroit Institute of Arts (1922) and the Folger Shakespeare Library in Washington, D.C. (1932). Both were marked by a spare interpretation of traditional forms and lean sculptural programs that earned Cret's architecture the description of "stripped classicism." As Cret's biographer Elizabeth Greenwell Grossman notes, his "impeccable sense of proportion gave his architecture an ineffable aura of both monumentality and intimacy unique in American civic architecture."[9]

Cret's work marked an elegant but somewhat tragic point of transition from centuries of stately monuments in stone and brick to the emerging era

FIGURE 5. The French-born architect Paul Philippe Cret, formerly of the École des Beaux-Arts in Paris, who became Kahn's most influential teacher and mentor at Penn. (Paul Philippe Cret Collection, The Architectural Archives, University of Pennsylvania)

of modern architectural technology based on steel, glass, and concrete. Until he was eclipsed by the arrival of European modernism under the leadership of such émigrés as Walter Gropius and Marcel Breuer in the late 1930s, Cret was among America's most prominent designers, winning the major awards in the profession, including the Gold Medal of the American Institute of Architects in 1938. Kahn studied under Cret for only his last year at Penn, and according to his transcript he was a good but not outstanding student; he was briefly on academic probation, and the school's top prizes went to others. But the combination of "monumentality and intimacy" in Cret's work became a defining aspect of his own architecture, and

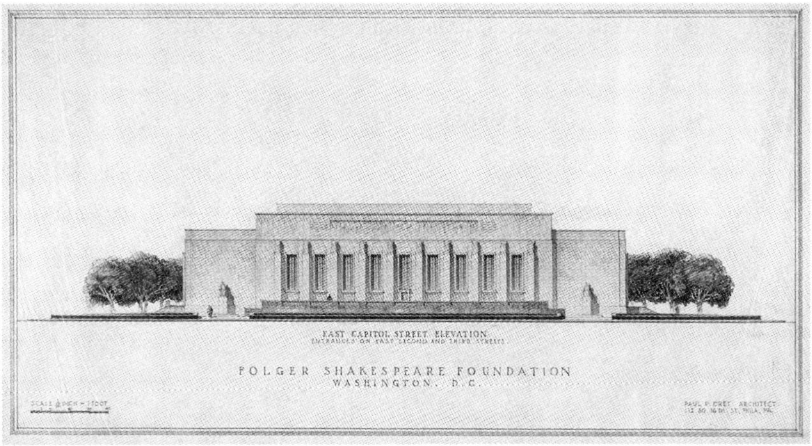

FIGURE 6. A rendering by Cret's office of his design for the Folger Shakespeare Library in Washington, D.C. (1932). (Used by permission of the Folger Shakespeare Library)

Kahn regarded his teacher as both a source of professional wisdom and personal support. According to Alexandra Tyng, Cret—who was the student adviser to Penn's Architecture Honorary Society—was possibly the reason Kahn was the first Jew to be admitted to an organization that normally excluded minorities.[10]

Family members and colleagues remember that Kahn never dwelled on his origins, and that he never complained about his social and physical deficits. But even a passing familiarity with psychology would suggest that as a mature man he was affected by the facts of his youth and education. He began his life in the United States as a poor, foreign, physically disfigured member of a religious minority that was looked down upon even by more established members of his own faith. He grew up in a city which, for all its humanistic traditions, was dominated by a powerful Christian establishment. And he chose a profession dominated by people who were most often Protestant, well-born, well-educated, and wealthy. For some aspiring architects, such origins might have resulted in anger, resentment, rebellion, and failure. Instead, they fueled a career of artistic triumph, and a unique legacy that has survived successive stylistic and ideological challenges.

TWO | SHOCK TO THE SYSTEM

Kahn finished his Penn education at a time of widespread optimism in the United States. American military forces had turned the tide of victory in the Great War, and the country had emerged from the conflict as the world's dominant industrial and military power. The income tax was only eleven years old, and the Roaring Twenties were still in full swing. As F. Scott Fitzgerald memorably described Tom and Daisy Buchanan and their ilk in *The Great Gatsby,* those at the top of American society were able to travel and gather "wherever people played polo and were rich together."

But if the United States was wealthy and powerful on the great scale, it was at some levels increasingly unstable. The young Union of Soviet Socialist Republics, established in 1922 in the wake of the Russian Revolution, had not yet fully revealed its totalitarian essence, and seemed to offer a brighter political future for the world's masses — at least many American intellectuals and artists thought so. As the historian Daniel Aaron described the climate of the times, Russia "stood for struggle, for joy, for the new day. . . . Here was a great country achieving remarkable gains under impossible conditions."[1] Among the American supporters of the Soviet experiment were such prominent writers as Max Eastman and John Reed, the activist and author of *Ten Days that Shook the World,* an account of the 1917 revolution. Though the playwright Arthur Miller, author of *The Crucible* and *Death of a Salesman,* among other literary classics, never joined the Communist Party, his biographer Martin Gottfried has observed that Miller, whose father had been wiped out financially on Wall Street, "was already angry with what America's economic system had done to his family. Extending those convictions to include an admiration for the Soviet Union probably seemed natural."[2] Miller and the renowned film director Elia Kazan (*On the Waterfront, Viva Zapata*), who *did* join the party, would famously fall out during the McCarthy era over their political differences, but as young men they and thousands of progressive Americans like them felt that the Soviets had found a way to cure the ills of capitalism. Louis Kahn never carried a party card, but as a survivor of Russia's imperial oppression and the ghettos of Philadelphia, he might be forgiven for sympathizing with the goals of improving the lot of the common man.

At the same time, the architectural profession was feeling the first ripples of seismic change in Europe. The physical and economic devastation left by the Great War had created an urgent need for housing, not only in areas directly affected by the fighting, but also in the cities where growing populations were strained by expanding industrialization. Le Corbusier had published his *Vers une Architecture* (*Towards a New Architecture*) in Paris in 1923, laying out a program for social uplift with an aesthetic foundation. "The Architect," he declared, "by his arrangement of forms, realizes an order which is a pure creation of his spirit . . . he determines the various movements of our heart and of our understanding; it is then that we experience the sense of beauty."[3] Those sentiments might have been expressed by any architect since Vitruvius; what made Le Corbusier's approach revolutionary was his declaration that "we shall arrive at the 'House-Machine,' the mass-production house, healthy (and morally so, too) and beautiful in the same way that the working tools and instruments which accompany our existence are beautiful."[4] Comparably radical views were being expressed in Germany and Holland.

All this must have been a potent brew for a young American architect whose family had experienced many of the evils of the "Old Order," in both

FIGURE 7. The Swiss-French architect Le Corbusier, whose pioneering modernism overwhelmed the Beaux-Arts tradition in which Kahn had been trained. (Fondation Le Corbusier/Artists Rights Society [ARS], New York)

Europe and America. But with the onset of the Great Depression in 1929, what had seemed to be America's unstoppable momentum abruptly stalled. More than five thousand banks closed, industrial production fell by half, and by 1933 between one-quarter and one-third of American workers were out of work.

Nevertheless, hope endured, especially after the election of Franklin Roosevelt to the presidency in 1933. The package of legislation that came to be known as the New Deal began to rekindle confidence in America's purpose and possibilities—and not a moment too soon. According to the historian Howard Zinn, the New Deal's organization of the economy was aimed partly at "giving enough help to the lower classes to keep them from turning a rebellion into a real revolution."[5] The restored optimism extended to the architecture academy with Walter Gropius, the former director of Germany's pioneering Bauhaus school, at the vanguard. Gropius had left his own country during the rise of the Nazis, bringing with him a powerful faith in the role of design in social uplift. The Bauhaus offered programs in painting, architecture, industrial design, graphic and fabric art, and photography, teaching that design should not be divided into isolated disciplines, but rather conceived as an integrated aesthetic whole with the goal of improving society. Among its members were such distinguished figures as Wassily Kandinsky, Paul Klee, and Josef Albers.

Having moved first to England, Gropius arrived at Harvard's Graduate School of Design in 1937, becoming chairman of the architecture department a year later. Gropius was soon followed by his Hungarian-born colleague Marcel Breuer who, like Gropius, went on to become one of the

FIGURE 8. The Bauhaus founder Walter Gropius, who revolutionized the Harvard architecture program. (HUP Gropius, Walter [4], Harvard University Archives)

dominant figures of American modernism. Reflecting on the goals of the Bauhaus just before reaching America, Gropius noted that "our ambition was to rouse the creative artist from his other-worldliness and reintegrate him into the workaday world of realities; and at the same time to broaden and humanize the rigid, almost exclusively material, mind of the businessman."[6] It is hard now to recapture the heady idealism of those days, but it was almost painfully intense. One Harvard architecture student, a classmate of the architect I. M. Pei who, like Pei, also studied under both Gropius and Breuer, spoke for a generation of his youthful colleagues when he declared, "We were going to change the world!"[7]

But some members of the profession saw less social uplift than cosmetic opportunity in the new design direction. The landmark 1932 exhibit, "The International Style," organized by Philip Johnson and Henry-Russell Hitchcock at New York's Museum of Modern Art, had laid out a new way of looking at and thinking about architecture. Hitchcock and Johnson celebrated the revolutionary developments in Europe, but focused less on the movement's goals of improving living conditions for the working class than on its aesthetics—the spare forms and new materials—which they saw as a "cleansing" of the heavily ornamented eclecticism of the recent past. In the book generated by the exhibition, Hitchcock and Johnson explained what had attracted their interest in what was happening across the Atlantic: "There is, first a new conception of architecture as volume rather than as mass. Secondly, regularity rather than axial symmetry serves as the chief means of ordering design. These two principles, with a third proscribing arbitrary applied decoration, mark the productions of the international style."[8] In assessing the work of the Dutch modernist architect J. J. P. Oud, the authors sounded a note that verged on the messianic: "The avoidance of picturesqueness, the severe horizontality of the composition, the perfect simplicity and consistency which he achieved in executing a very complex project, all announced the conscious creation of a body of aesthetic disciplines."[9] The choice of words—severe, perfect, disciplines—revealed an almost puritanical reaction to the perceived "sins" of the past.

American institutions and corporations gradually took notice, realizing that buildings designed in the new style were far easier and less expensive to build than the ornate masonry masses that had anchored American cities, whose marble banks and limestone courthouses were intended to create confidence in tradition. Compounding the financial crisis, the change in style meant that the market for those grand civic monuments—the very architecture which Kahn had been trained to revere—rapidly evaporated.

Among the professional casualties of this new direction were most of the leading figures of traditional American architecture, including Cass Gilbert (who designed the Supreme Court building in Washington, D.C.), Charles Klauder (who created the University of Pittsburgh's Cathedral of Learning), Horace Trumbauer (who conceived Harvard's Widener Library), and scores of other once-celebrated architectural names that are now mostly lost to history. Surely the most eloquent protest against what was happening was voiced by Ralph Adams Cram, the American dean of the English neo-Gothic, master planner of Princeton University's campus, and designer of the Cadet Chapel at West Point. In his autobiography, *My Life in Architecture,* Cram wrote that modernism "has its own place and it may and should go to it. Its boundaries are definite and fixed, and beyond them it cannot go, for the Angel of Decency, Propriety, and Reason stands there with a flaming sword."[10]

All this must have left Louis Kahn feeling professionally and artistically unhinged. The Beaux-Arts–based architecture in which he had been schooled was slipping out of fashion, and the financial boom that was to have sustained it into the future had collapsed. Fortunately, he secured a position as a draftsman with John Molitor, the city architect of Philadelphia, and was soon promoted and put in charge of overseeing the design of the buildings for the Philadelphia Sesquicentennial Exhibition, planned for 1926. The classically inspired scheme drew on Kahn's Beaux-Arts training, but as such it had little to do with the new trends in architecture. Neither did his work in 1927 and 1928 for the Philadelphia architect William H. Lee, an architect and theater designer.

Even before finishing up at Penn, Kahn had been putting money aside for a trip to Europe to see the major monuments. He left Lee's office in the spring of 1928, and spent the next year traveling through England, Holland, and Germany, taking time out for a visit to his family's former home in Estonia. His version of the traditional Grand Tour exposed him to the great works of western European architectural history as no academic course at Penn could have done. The drawings Kahn made using pencil and black crayon in England at the beginning of his trip are sober and largely representational, the architectural details picked out with the sort of academic precision that he had clearly demonstrated as a student. His style changed dramatically when he moved on to Italy. There, he developed a much more abstract approach, recording mass more than detail and reducing his concentration on specifics in favor of simple, even blunt, strokes emphasizing the architectonic massing of his subjects. Based on the profusion of drawings and paintings Kahn produced in Italy, and the evident change in his style from detailed to abstract, it is clear that his visits to the towers of San Gimignano, to the brooding temples of Paestum, and to the other works, both great and humble, that he observed there marked a fundamental shift in his way of seeing.

During Kahn's stay in Paris, he met up with Norman Rice, a fellow Penn architecture graduate who was the first American architect to work with Le Corbusier. Curiously, Kahn did not exploit his classmate's connection to meet the architect who was emerging as a standard-bearer of the new modernism. But a young American architect promenading on the Champs Élysées, sipping wine with a friend and convert to radical modernism, could not have avoided the clash of tradition and change that was consuming his art and profession.

FIGURE 9. Newlyweds Louis Kahn and Esther Israeli. (Esther Kahn Collection, The Architectural Archives, University of Pennsylvania)

That clash, taking place at such a formative stage of Kahn's life (he was only twenty-seven), is likely to have set him thinking about the relative merits of architecture's past and its future. Kahn would never fit a neat characterization as a traditionalist or a revolutionary. Surely one reason is that his personal history, his education, and his travels had positioned him to profit from everything he had experienced. Architectural history, informed by change and concern for those affected by both, would guide his every step as a mature architect.

When Kahn returned to Philadelphia from Europe, he resumed a romantic relationship that had started at a party at Penn in the late 1920s, when he was introduced to Esther Israeli, an elegant young Penn alumna who was pursuing a master's degree in experimental psychology. They were married on August 14, 1930, but because the economy was still in crisis, ended up moving in with Esther's parents at 5243 Chester Avenue in Philadelphia, living on the third floor. Kahn contributed to the household expenses through a small income from work with his former mentor, Paul Cret. But when Cret developed throat cancer his practice declined, leaving Kahn without the career that had seemed so promising only a few years earlier. The setback must have been frustrating, but it was only temporary.

THREE | KEEPING THE FAITH

As the effects of the Depression spread grimly across the country, the Roosevelt administration responded with a massive campaign of economic policies and public-works projects that came to be known as the New Deal. While the proliferation of these programs (which included the Civilian Conservation Corps, the Works Progress Administration, and the Tennessee Valley Authority) were practical reactions to a national emergency, and put hundreds of thousands of Americans back to work, they had in common the idealistic theme of social responsibility. Faced with bread lines in Chicago, near-starvation in the Dust Bowl of the Midwest, shanty towns in New York's Central Park, and the looming prospect of national economic collapse, many Americans came together in a spirit of sacrifice. Although the well-born Roosevelt's programs were fiercely criticized in politically conservative quarters as a form of socialism (FDR was widely attacked by his fellow graduates of Groton and Harvard as a "traitor to his class"), they nonetheless found especially fertile ground in Philadelphia, with its tradition of community service.

They certainly met with a warm reception from Louis Kahn. In 1930, left unemployed following the closing of Cret's firm, he struggled to locate work of almost any kind. So dire were his straits that he applied in that year to design of one of the country's humbler building types: a gas station. While the idea might have seemed far-fetched for an architect of Kahn's training, it could be seen not solely as a matter of financial desperation, but also as conforming to his emerging commitment to social betterment. After all, the

FIGURE 10. A shantytown spawned by the Great Depression in New York's Central Park, about 1931. (Everett Collection Historical/Alamy Stock Photo)

automobile had come to define American life, and enhancing the aesthetics of a proliferating building type may have seemed like a worthy undertaking, especially if it paid the bills. While the client, Shell Petroleum, was grateful for the proposal (Kahn had already written them three previous letters), acknowledging that "we fully appreciate that there are, undoubtedly, improvements to be made in our station design," it gently rebuffed Kahn's appeal. In his response, Shell's manager of operations concluded, "We thank you for your interest but it would not be worth your time to develop the matter further with us."[1]

Kahn subsequently managed to secure brief employment with the local architecture firm of Zantzinger, Borie and Medary, the architects of the 1928 Philadelphia Museum of Art. His assignment was to develop plans for the Justice Department Building in Washington, D.C., which required him to live in the capital during the week. Nevertheless, in early 1932, the deepening financial crisis forced the firm to let him go, evidently with regret. In his letter to Kahn, Clarence Zantzinger noted, "We take this opportunity of expressing to you our appreciation of the character of work that you have so well performed for us during your term in this office."[2] Undeterred, Kahn turned his creative energies to rallying his unemployed colleagues. His new wife was sympathetic, but anxious. On July 18, 1931, Esther confided in her diary, "Our days are filled with work we like, and our evenings with work of our own at home . . . Louis says I mope — I do, but only about money. This problem is quite a large one."[3]

Although without a job, and financially dependent on his wife and her parents, Kahn remained dedicated to his evolving architectural mission, and in January of 1933 he carried his concerns back to his former school. In a lecture entitled "Architecture and Modern Housing," prepared for the students of the University of Pennsylvania architecture program, he insisted that architects "can contribute to the good life not only in the ordinary sense of providing beauty for people to see, but also by producing projects which they believe tend to advance the common good in other ways — things, for instance, that promote good economics, rather than socially destructive projects like Radio City, which, even if successful to its financial backers, will probably hurt the rest of the community."[4] Architects, he insisted, "can do society great good." Kahn's jab at the entertainment centerpiece of New York's Rockefeller Center was further — if condescending — evidence of his commitment to what he considered to be architecture's higher purpose.

Central to the conversation among progressive Philadelphia architects at the time was the *T-Square Journal of Philadelphia,* a magazine supported by the prominent local architect George Howe, who had launched it in 1930. Although it lasted only two years, the publication encouraged idealistic debate about the role of architecture in meeting the crisis presented by the Depression. Howe, a handsome, Harvard-educated and Beaux-Arts–trained patrician, had spent his early career designing romantic country estates based on European models for the Philadelphia gentry. Among his best-known creations was High Hollow, the residence he designed for himself in Chestnut Hill, finished in 1914. Based on the thesis he had presented at the Ecole in Paris, it was a sumptuous mix of Italian and French sources, built of brick and stone, with balconies, an ornamental pool, and a tennis court. According to Howe's biographer, Robert A. M. Stern, High Hollow "established the standard for fashionable country house design around Philadelphia for the next twenty years."[5] Although the building, which was set in a suburban Philadelphia landscape vaguely reminiscent of northern Italy, was overtly romantic and stylistically retrospective, it showed a sensitivity to detail and siting and hinted at a frustration with the literally imitative architecture favored by many prosperous Americans at that time for their country retreats.

FIGURE 11. The aristocratic architect George Howe, Kahn's first and lasting patron. (Athenaeum of Philadelphia, Mellor, Meigs & Howe Collection)

Howe eventually became a partner in the Philadelphia firm of Mellor, Meigs and Howe, but for all his traditional training and financial success, he began to drift toward more modern forms and finally set out on his own. What amounted to a radical aesthetic conversion accelerated in the late 1920s, when Howe met a Swiss-born architect named William Lescaze. As a student in Zurich, Lescaze had been exposed to the early strains of modernist design, which he brought with him when he came to America in 1920. Through a mutual friend, he was introduced to Howe, who had secured a

FIGURE 12. Howe's romantically retrograde Pennsylvania residence, High Hollow (1916). (Chestnut Hill Conservancy)

commission to design a building for the Philadelphia Saving Fund Society (PSFS) and was struggling to find a form that would move beyond the traditional Greek columns, Roman vaults, and Renaissance rustication normally associated with banks. (One of Howe's early efforts had included Gothic piers.) Howe found a kindred spirit in Lescaze, with whom he formed a partnership in 1929. Lescaze brought with him the latest in European architectural advances, and with Howe's social and business connections the pair combined precisely the credentials required for the assignment. Their landmark high-rise, completed in 1932, was a sleek glass-and-steel tower

FIGURE 13. The pathbreaking Philadelphia Saving Fund Society tower, by Howe and the Swiss modernist William Lescaze (1931). (Philadelphia Saving Fund Society records [accession 2062], HagleyID 20100224_305, Hagley Museum and Library)

unlike anything seen before in America, combining banking rooms, offices, and retail stores.

Meanwhile, *T-Square* was publishing essays by such contributors as R. Buckminster Fuller (the future inventor of the geodesic dome), Raymond Hood (later a principal architect of Rockefeller Center), Ely Jacques Kahn, Richard Neutra, and even Frank Lloyd Wright. As is often the case in times of economic stress and low employment, intellectual activity flourished, in this case focused on how architecture could assist in battling the effects of the Depression. Howe knew of Kahn's work, and invited him to contribute an essay, which he happily did, entitling it "The Value and Aim in Sketching." But the connection between the men soon expanded well beyond Howe's struggling journal, and was to prove catalytic for both.

On the face of it, the relationship was an odd one, but as their time together increased, each man seemed to provide the other with something he felt was lacking. Howe—with his pince-nez spectacles, bow ties, and silver flask—was as close to an American aristocrat as one could imagine, but he was always candid about his creative limitations. Kahn could not have been more of an outsider in Howe's social circle, but his up-from-nothing authenticity and his creative potential must have been evident to his friend, who was mature enough to admire talent rather than envy it. Kahn's daughter Alexandra recalled her father describing a day when he and Howe were riding in an elevator. Kahn reportedly told Howe how much he admired his bow tie, at which point Howe stripped it off and presented it to him. (This became Kahn's signature neckwear.) For a man of Howe's proper bearing, it was a remarkably intimate gesture.[6]

Amplifying the efforts of the magazine, Kahn helped found a discussion group, first named the Society for the Advancement of Architecture and later rechristened as the Architectural Research Group (ARG), which convened weekly at a local restaurant. In the draft preamble setting forth the group's "principles and practices," written in April of 1933, the members observed that "architecture should be the visual resultant [*sic*] of the manifold cooperations [*sic*] of thought, social relations, biological activities, and cosmic backgrounds of a civilization." Among the group's objectives was to investigate "the most advanced ideas of architecture based upon the needs of man and his activities, and to attempt to anticipate the point of view."[7] An ARG proposal to the City of Philadelphia on "slum clearance" listed among its goals not only "a better city," but also "a more contented population."[8] However naïve the platform of the ARG may seem by today's standards, its high-minded goals were achingly sincere. They did not, however, pay the bills. According to Esther Kahn, some of the ARG's members left to pursue work in other professions, but, as she remembered, "Lou would never give up architecture."[9]

A frequent topic of discussion at the ARG meetings was the growing crisis of homelessness spawned by the Depression. Although low-cost housing had been at the center of the European modernist movement, it had not attracted much attention in America. Such prominent social critics as Lewis Mumford and Catherine Bauer lamented the lack of low-cost, high-quality housing in the United States, noting that "Europe has millions of low-rental, high-standard, modern dwellings in communities planned carefully to provide a maximum of amenity, pleasantness, efficiency, and long-time economy."[10] The Depression had begun to change that. Indeed, among the first American versions of the European-style mass-housing effort were the Carl Mackley Houses, designed for textile workers in Philadelphia under FDR's Public Works Administration by Oscar Stonorov and Alfred Kastner, recent immigrants from Germany who had won second place in the 1931 competition for the Palace of the Soviets in Moscow. The architects' previous interest in the Soviet Union was not yet a cause for political alarm in America, where most progressive designers and intellectuals were still drawn to the Russian experiment in social uplift. The Mackley Houses reflected the current design trends in Europe: buildings organized in rows with flat roofs and strip windows. Although hardly striking from an aesthetic point of view, the development included garages and a swimming pool, amenities unheard of until then for American blue-collar workers.

In Kahn's case, the Soviet link was strong. Surely the most colorful project on which Kahn worked during this period was a competition in 1933 for a monument to Vladimir Lenin to be erected in Leningrad. The ARG's application waxed eloquent about the design, describing it as centered on "two great towers of red glass" located above a plaza at the edge of the city's harbor. The plaza was to be "enclosed by two sculptural arms of stone whereon is depicted the epochal emergence of the Proletariat and the Peasant—from Exploitation, through Struggle, to Victory and Achievement."[11] The project was not selected, and it was not an effort Kahn highlighted later in life, most likely because of the anti-Communist wave that swept the country during the so-called McCarthy era in the 1950s. Nevertheless, it was thoroughly consistent with his political views at the time, not to mention his need for financial support.

For all his activism, Kahn had still not become a registered architect. On July 12, 1934, he made a formal application to the Pennsylvania State Board of Examiners of Architects, citing his work with Molitor on the Sesquicentennial Exposition. One of his supporters, Bernard Newman, managing director of the Philadelphia Housing Association, with whom Kahn had worked, submitted a letter of recommendation describing Kahn as "the most promising of this younger group with whose work we are familiar."[12] Nevertheless, the examiners responded in August that, because of "a general lack of clear understanding of most of the questions asked," the Board "cannot grant you a certificate of qualification and registration based on the questions as answered by you." Reflecting Kahn's perilous financial situation, the rejection was made more painful when the board returned the check for $25 that Kahn had included to cover the application fee. The check, they noted, "was returned to us by the State Treasurer's Office, inasmuch as they were unable to cash the same."[13] The young architect pressed on, and in May of the following year he received an encouraging letter from the same Bernard Newman who had backed him a year earlier. "Congratulations on having passed your State Board," Newman wrote. "If you will keep on being as practical and yet as ingenious as you have already shown yourself to be, we shall see big things from you."[14]

Kahn's prospects began to improve when Kastner invited him in 1935 to join in the design of a low-cost housing project called Jersey Homesteads. The aim of the project was to relocate some two hundred garment workers and their families from the tenements of New York City to suburban New Jersey. Underlying the simple provision of better-quality housing units in a healthier environment was a commitment to communal identity. Indeed, the moving force behind Jersey Homesteads, Benjamin Brown, was an advocate of the so-called back-to-the-land movement, and the original scheme included a school, community center, cooperative farm, and clothing factory intended to make the complex largely self-sufficient. Engaging as the Homesteads planning must have been for an architect with sympathy for the underprivileged, Kahn's involvement did not last long, and he was laid off in early 1937.

Kahn got a measure of relief with the commission for the Ahaveth Israel Synagogue in Philadelphia. While Kahn never considered himself an observant Jew, his connections to Philadelphia's Jewish artistic and politically progressive community made him an obvious candidate for any such assignment. This building was little more than a brick box presenting a largely blank façade to the street, but it marked the beginning of Kahn's institutional work and may have given him a taste of designing for programs beyond the merely practical.

Although steadied by his professional license, the synagogue commission, and his work with Kastner, Kahn was by no means stable financially. A stint as a consulting architect in 1937 with the Philadelphia Housing Authority did not do much to improve the situation. As Esther noted in her journal in February of 1937, "Lou is not discouraged. I feel that he may soon begin to be recognized. He has such talent and ability, plus the enthusiasm and desire for his profession that he will get ahead. But I hope it will be soon."[15]

The outbreak of World War II did much to stimulate the economy, but

FIGURE 14. Kahn's low-cost Carver Court worker-housing project in Pennsylvania (1944). (Gottscho-Schleisner Collection, Library of Congress)

it also increased the need for low-cost housing to accommodate workers in war industries and thereafter for soldiers returning from overseas. Working with Howe and Oscar Stonorov, Kahn embarked on the design of Carver Court in 1941, a project with one hundred units intended for steelworkers on a former racetrack outside Coatesville, Pennsylvania. The housing units were raised above ground, leaving room below for cars. Consistent with the socially responsible sentiments that the architects shared, the centerpiece of the development was a community center. Kahn and Stonorov went on to design seven more projects for industrial workers (Howe left the team in 1944 to head the Public Buildings Administration in Washington, D.C.), and five were completed. The progressive aspects of these developments, and especially Carver Court, afforded the architects a prominent place in an exhibition at the Museum of Modern Art entitled *Built in the USA, 1932–1944*.

While the socially redeeming value of low-cost housing design must have been satisfying to Kahn on many levels, allowing him to pursue the goals of the ARG and "advance the common good" as he had urged students at Penn to do in his speech in 1933, something was missing, even apart from money. In 1943, Kahn and Stonorov wrote two widely circulated pamphlets whose titles suggest an evolving focus: "Why City Planning Is Your Responsibility" and "You and Your Neighborhood: A Primer for Neighborhood Planning." A year later, however, Kahn wrote a polemical essay entitled simply "Monumentality." In it, he hinted at the frustration and the ambition that were evidently altering his concentration. "Monumentality in architecture," he wrote, "may be defined as a quality, a spiritual quality inherent in a structure which conveys the feeling of its eternity, that it cannot be added to or changed." He went on to pose a question that linked his social idealism to his aesthetic ambitions: "But have we yet given full architectural expression to such social monuments as the school, the community, or culture center?"[16]

This was not about size, but about impact, and meaning. Kahn may have been wondering whether housing for masses of low-income workers was the most efficient way to fulfill his idealistic goals. His frustration seems to have coincided with a change in his understanding of modernist design. As the historian Joseph Rykwert has noted, there was at the time a growing interest in the possibility of a new kind of architecture "that was not historically conditioned but grew out of the best of the avant-garde work of the 1930s." According to Rykwert, this sensibility "marked the end of the purely utilitarian, 'functionalist' view of modernity."[17] Kahn's frustration would find release in the next phase of his career, which began with his appointment as a visiting critic in Yale's Department of Architecture. The new position, which involved traveling from Philadelphia to New Haven two days a week, exposed him to a powerful array of artistic talent. It was an eclectic environment that perfectly suited Kahn as he sorted out his own Beaux-Arts training and the imperatives of modern design and social responsibility.

FOUR | RIGHT TIME, RIGHT PLACE

Louis Kahn's arrival in New Haven, Connecticut, in 1947 as a member of the faculty of the Yale Department of Architecture was almost accidental. Yale had been hoping to hire Oscar Niemeyer, the distinguished Brazilian modernist architect who had participated (with Le Corbusier, Wallace Harrison, and others) in planning the United Nations headquarters building in New York City, as a visiting critic. But as the postwar Red Scare over the Soviet Union's expanding influence spread, Niemeyer was blocked from returning to the United States due to government concerns about his Communist affiliations.

Denied his first choice, the department's chairman, Harold Hauf, contacted Louis Kahn, whose work he knew largely through Kahn's publications on housing. As it turned out, the Brazilian star's diplomatic misfortune created a transformative opportunity for the relatively obscure forty-six-year-old American. While by now an established authority in the area of public- and low-cost housing, Kahn was not otherwise widely known in the American architectural community. Moreover, even though he had recently separated professionally from Oscar Stonorov and opened his own office, he had little exposure to the architectural or social circles outside his still rather provincial Philadelphia. He remained, however, intensely devoted to art and music, having narrowly chosen architecture as a calling, and Yale was unique among American universities at the time in its offerings in those areas. Indeed, as the architect and historian Robert A. M. Stern (dean of the Yale School of Architecture from 1998–2016) has noted,

FIGURE 15. Chapel Street in New Haven, Connecticut, showing Street Hall (*on right*) and the Old Art Gallery. (Manuscripts and Archives, Yale University Library)

Yale's School of the Fine Arts, which then included the Department of Architecture, was established on the principle that "the ideal of teaching the various arts was pursued in the belief that studying painting, sculpture, and architecture side by side had distinct advantages."[1] Kahn's appointment gave him a chance to indulge all of his passions. Beyond that, however, it marked the first step on his journey from an advocate of social uplift to a shaper of culture on what would become a global scale.

Kahn could not have arrived in New Haven at a better time. Yale was the first college in America to establish an art school, and from its founding in

1869 the School of Fine Arts displayed an independent streak, most noticeably by accepting women. The Department of Architecture was established as part of the school in 1916.

The influence of art in Kahn's Yale experience seems to have been transformative. Programs in architecture at other American universities were usually located in schools of engineering, archaeology, or applied science. Yale, by contrast, saw itself as a champion of aesthetics. Apart from its traditional identity as a college devoted to the humanities, Yale—which since its founding in 1701 had added schools of divinity, law, and medicine, and was designated a university in 1887—offered a unique combination of postgraduate resources in the arts. Its music department, with a faculty that included the German-born avant-garde composer Paul Hindemith, competed with such prominent institutions as Juilliard in New York and Curtis in Philadelphia; its drama department was a leader in its field; and the graduate program in art included such teachers as Jack Tworkov, the pioneering abstract expressionist Willem de Kooning, and the sculptor Robert Engman. Beyond these programs, the university faculty boasted such cross-disciplinary thinkers as Paul Weiss. A prominent member of Yale's philosophy department, and Yale's first Jewish full professor, Weiss ranged well beyond his traditional area of study into theology and cosmology, with an especially strong interest in art and its relationship to the rest of the human condition. In one of his books, he noted that "my approach to art, through the thick of experience, has been accompanied by a reflection on its nature, provoked, guided, and supported by speculations into the essence of existence, freedom and the place that art has among the primary disciplines."[2] Although he remained religiously nonobservant, Kahn became increasingly drawn to the connections between architecture and spirituality. Whether it was a result of that emerging affinity, or the fact that he and Weiss were both short in stature and among the few Jews at the university, they would

FIGURE 16. The Yale philosophy professor Paul Weiss, whose scholarship embraced art and architecture. (Manuscripts and Archives, Yale University Library)

become friends as well as academic colleagues. Although officially an outsider, Weiss became a regular visitor at the architecture department's design reviews.

In the late 1940s, Yale was a relatively small institution located in a small city, so the interaction among students and faculty was easier and more frequent than it might have been in New York City or Boston. The smoky Sullivan's Bar and the neon-lit Waldorf Cafeteria, both located on Chapel Street not far from the architecture department, became centers of intellectual interaction and artistic debate, one fueled largely by alcohol, the other by coffee, but both acting as offsite classrooms. Kahn and Weiss were especially fond of the Waldorf, which was open well into the night. Whatever the location, the combination of disciplines and personalities produced a uniquely creative ferment.

There was similarly a remarkable mix of influences in the architecture department itself. When Kahn took up his position at Yale as a critic, his colleagues included such prominent talents as Wallace Harrison, a veteran of the United Nations design team; Philip Johnson, who was already at work on his soon-to-be-famous Glass House in New Canaan, Connecticut; Eero Saarinen, who later designed the TWA terminal at Idlewild (now JFK) Airport in New York and the Gateway Arch in St. Louis; Pietro Belluschi, later dean of the architecture school at MIT; and Hugh Stubbins, later designer of the innovative Citicorp Center in New York City.

By 1949, Kahn had risen to the rank of Yale's chief critic, and when Harold Hauf resigned as department chairman to become editor of *Architec-*

tural Record, Kahn urged Charles Sawyer, who was then dean of the School of the Fine Arts, to approach George Howe, his former Philadelphia mentor and partner, to fill the position.

But Howe was far away and likely out of the running. In 1942, as part of the war effort, he had been appointed supervising architect of the Public Buildings Administration, the highest government position for an architect. A year later he became the first modernist architect to be made a fellow of the American Institute of Architects. Howe is credited with moving the design of government buildings away from the stripped classicism of Kahn's mentor Paul Cret and his followers toward a more modern vocabulary. But the Washington bureaucracy left him little room for creativity. Howe resigned from his government post in 1945 and in 1947 became resident architect at the American Academy in Rome, looking forward to a graceful retirement.

Established in 1894 by a group of American artists and architects who had worked on the 1893 World's Columbian Exposition in Chicago, and led by Charles Follen McKim of the renowned firm of McKim, Mead and White, the Rome academy was intended to be a place where American scholars and artists from all disciplines could immerse themselves in the classical tradition. Although Howe was one of the early American modernist architects, he was still a Beaux-Arts alumnus and had never lost his affection for traditional European architecture. Even after two years in Rome he was still enjoying the European experience.

But Charles Sawyer persisted. Well aware that Kahn and Howe had been colleagues in Philadelphia, Sawyer increased the pressure. With the help of his faculty colleague Edward Durell Stone, Kahn pressed Howe to take the job. Kahn wrote to him, stating in forceful terms, "George, the school needs your personality and your kind of leadership," noting that "the school is progressive, and in the state of constant change and development. There is no dictation from above. Everyone seems to like the results although there is no particular order or ideology followed."[3] A loyal alumnus of Harvard College, Howe wrote to his daughter, "Isn't that a break? If you had asked me which school I would like to head I'd have picked Yale."[4] He accepted the offer and took over the Yale department on January 1, 1950.

One of Howe's earliest concerns was to distinguish the Yale program from Harvard's. Since its founding in 1895, the latter's architecture program had reflected the familiar model established by the Ecole des Beaux-Arts and followed by such schools as Columbia and Kahn's alma mater, the University of Pennsylvania. Then in 1935, Harvard hired Joseph Hudnut, the architecture dean at Columbia, to take over the program in Cambridge. Branching off dramatically from his Columbia roots, Hudnut proceeded to consolidate Harvard's programs in architecture, landscape design, and urban planning into what became known as the Graduate School of Design (GSD). In 1937, Hudnut hired the Bauhaus founder Walter Gropius, who had recently arrived in the United States after a two-year stopover in England on his self-imposed exile from Nazi Germany. Together they undertook a thorough reorganization of the GSD curriculum.

Most significant for Yale, Hudnut and Gropius radically deemphasized courses involving history and the arts. Reflecting on the mission of the Bauhaus, which became in slightly altered form that of the GSD, Gropius asserted that "a breach has been made with the past, which allows us to envisage a new aspect of architecture corresponding to the technical civilization of the age we live in; the morphology of dead styles has been destroyed; and we are returning to honesty of thought and feeling."[5] To emphasize the change in direction, Gropius and Hudnut transferred the study of architectural history out of the GSD and relegated those courses and all the classical plaster casts, from which architecture students had traditionally learned to draw, to Harvard College. As the historian Anthony Alofsin observes in his history of the Harvard architecture program, "In simplified terms, the GSD of 1937 saw that the old school reveled in architecture as art over technol-

FIGURE 17. Josef Albers, the Bauhaus alumnus and founder of Yale's graphic arts program, in his studio in New Haven, May 1954. (Yale Events and Activities Photographs [RU 690], Manuscripts and Archives, Yale University Library; Charles Alburtus, photographer)

ogy; in the new school, architecture served a social purpose, even if that social purpose was often a generalized and vague goal rather than a specific program."[6]

Since the origins of Yale's architecture program lay in the arts, it was not surprising that Howe chose to emphasize that tradition, especially since by the time he arrived in New Haven the doctrinaire approach of Harvard was beginning to erode due to faculty dissension.

Howe was joined in his efforts to redefine the Yale department by Josef Albers, a former colleague of Gropius who had studied painting under Paul Klee at the Bauhaus and who, like Gropius, had immigrated to the United States. Albers had been teaching at Black Mountain College in North Carolina, which opened in 1933, a radically experimental institution founded on a commitment to art as a fundamental component of a liberal arts education. At the heart of the college's philosophy was a belief in interdisciplinary and collaborative work. Although the college closed in 1957, it attracted a staggering array of faculty talent that included Gropius; Albers and his wife,

Anni, a leading textile artist; the choreographer Merce Cunningham; and the painters Franz Kline, Robert Motherwell, and Robert Rauschenberg.

While trained primarily as a painter, Albers had also designed furniture and became an advocate of the use of stained glass in architecture. When he became chairman of Yale's Department of Art in 1950, he brought with him all the interdisciplinary influences he had absorbed at the Bauhaus and at Black Mountain to New Haven. Albers arrived less than a year after Howe had assumed his position heading the Department of Architecture, and together they created a formidable alternative to the Harvard program of technology-based social improvement. In addition to Johnson, Saarinen, and Stone, the faculty included a less well-known figure, Eugene Nalle, whose original training had been in cabinetmaking, described by Howe as "a dedicated teacher, an artist-philosopher begotten by Yale out of carpentry and building."[7] Another prominent figure was the Chinese-born King-lui Wu, who taught an influential course entitled "Daylight and Architec-

FIGURE 18. The Yale art historian Vincent Scully, a charismatic teacher and early Kahn advocate. (Manuscripts and Archives, Yale University Library)

ture." They were joined by the city planning expert Christopher Tunnard, a Canadian who had trained as a landscape architect in England. Acting as a bridge to the art history department was the charismatic Vincent Scully, whose passionate lectures and devotion to a Jungian interpretation of architectural form mesmerized generations of students.

Even before Howe's arrival, Yale had been flirting with a departure from the path of traditional design, and acknowledged the changes in the profession by expanding its list of visitors; in 1935, both Frank Lloyd Wright and Le Corbusier had delivered guest lectures. Apart from its evolving academic offerings, however, Yale was the scene of memorable informal gatherings that included students and faculty from the departments of art, architecture, drama, and music, which became almost part of the curriculum. Herbert Newman, an architect who studied under Kahn at Yale, observed that "we felt profoundly the intermingling of the arts and architecture."[8] Another student, Ludovica Schniewind, came to know Albers and his wife socially, and although she never took a dedicated course with the students in Street Hall, the headquarters of the art department, she recalls that "we walked around their studios freely, and learned from their work."[9]

One of the formal ways in which that intermingling was encouraged was via what was called the collaborative problem, which engaged the school's architects, painters, and sculptors. The exercise had slipped into disuse, but was revived by Hauf in 1948, and Kahn took charge of it, creating sixteen teams, each of which included two architects, two painters, and a sculptor. Two representative projects included a "National Center for UNESCO," and "An Idea Center for Plastics." Perhaps the most memorable of the collaborative efforts was one led by the irreverent visiting faculty member R. Buckminster Fuller. A Harvard College dropout, Fuller was, like Albers, a Black Mountain veteran, and although he had limited formal training, he proved to be a visionary in the fields of architecture and engineering, most notably with the development of the geodesic dome, a lightweight but extremely strong structure assembled from prefabricated parts. Fuller's collaborative project for his Yale students involved the design of a thirty-foot dome constructed of cardboard on the roof of Weir Hall, the main architecture school building. Although the structure collapsed in a rainstorm, its mere creation was a historic event for the students who participated in it.

Although by this time Kahn occupied a senior position on the architecture faculty, he struck some of his colleagues as lacking an artistic focus. As Vincent Scully described the Beaux-Arts–trained Kahn at the time, "He was trying to be an International Style architect, and he couldn't be. He just didn't feel it that way, he couldn't make it that way."[10] Scully went on to observe, "It was clear that here was a man who'd lost an order and was looking for it everywhere. What the order was nobody knew. He didn't know himself, but he constantly talked about it."[11]

If Kahn was drifting in his professional life, his personal affairs were also unsteady. Although he'd been married since 1930, Kahn had begun an affair with a woman in his Philadelphia office named Anne Tyng. The daughter of American missionaries to China, where she had spent much of her youth, Tyng graduated from Radcliffe College with a degree in fine arts and became one of the first women at Harvard's Graduate School of Design. She had joined the Kahn and Stonorov office in 1945 and quickly became an influential member of the design team, bringing to it a fascination with the role of pure geometry in architecture. A romance with Kahn soon developed, and when Tyng became pregnant, she followed the usual practice of the time, leaving the country to avoid public embarrassment and have the child, a daughter she and Kahn named Alexandra. Heartfelt as Kahn's passionate letters to Tyng in Rome during her absence may have been, they masked an affair with another young employee, Marie Kuo, a relationship that continued following Tyng's return from Europe, and foreshadowed yet another major infidelity.

In 1950, Kahn had his own, and very different, reason for traveling to

Rome when he was invited to succeed Howe as a resident architect at the American Academy. In the three months he was abroad, from December of 1950 to February of 1951, Kahn was afforded an intense exposure to Rome's ancient ruins by Frank E. Brown, a Yale professor of archaeology who was serving as head of the academy's Classical School. Kahn also revisited many of the sites he had seen on his earlier trip, but this time he was able to range as far as Greece and Egypt. The brilliantly colored pastel drawings he sketched on his travels—especially those of the majestic temples in Athens and Karnak, and the pyramids at Giza—showed an emerging fascination with the enduring power of ancient monuments. Having missed the work of Le Corbusier in 1929, Kahn paid a visit to the Swiss-French architect's concrete landmark, the Unité d'Habitation, then under construction in Marseilles. Although brief, the trip clearly added to his rapid—if late—maturing as an architect.

On his return from Rome, Kahn resumed his teaching at Yale, but with fresh eyes. Although it is hard to document what seemed to be a consolidation of his sense of artistic purpose, Kahn's attitude toward the architecture of the Yale campus provides a clue. In the 1920s, the university had decided to radically rebuild its campus on the model of the ancient English universities of Cambridge and Oxford. Contributing to this decision was Yale's desire to create a tangible link to the scholarly traditions of those great centers of learning. The architect responsible for most of this effort was James Gamble Rogers, a graduate of Yale College who had studied architecture at the Ecole des Beaux-Arts and distinguished himself as one of the leading eclectics of his day, equally adept at designing buildings in the Gothic, classical, and Georgian styles. His signature Yale building was the 1921 Harkness Tower, a neo-Gothic spire at the heart of the campus (see color plate 2). Widely hailed by such prominent academic observers as the president of Harvard, it nonetheless offended virtually every architect sympathetic to the changing times. When Frank Lloyd Wright visited Yale, he was asked where he would like to stay. His famous reply was, "Harkness Tower, so I would not have to look at it."

It was easy in the 1940s to mock what was derided as the "stage-set" architecture of the Yale campus. After all, the Second World War had wrenched the United States violently into the modern era in virtually every dimension. But Kahn had a more nuanced reaction to the buildings that surrounded him in New Haven. Having trained under Cret in the Beaux-Arts tradition and then begun a personal transition, however reluctantly, to modernism in the 1930s, Kahn could not be expected to embrace the historically imitative architecture of the Yale campus. But according to Herbert Newman, Kahn saw beyond the stylistic lifting of Rogers's buildings to their "weight" and "solidity." Beyond that, Newman recalled that Kahn was impressed by the "intimacy" of the Yale residential colleges, all of which were centered on differentiated courtyards and inflected with irregular spaces designed to encourage both interaction among the students and a sense of group identity.[12]

Beyond those attributes, Kahn seems to have drawn a larger lesson from Yale's motivation in the design and execution of its historicist architecture. The institution was candid about its wish to create a link to the educational models on which its pedagogy was based. Just as the central grounds of Thomas Jefferson's University of Virginia were intended to expose its students to the political messages conveyed by Greek and Roman examples, Yale's campus was designed to encourage its students to associate themselves with the highest examples of transatlantic learning. By investing so heavily in the rich materials and fine details used in the residential colleges, Yale was not only displaying its wealth and power, but also reminding the young residents, however subliminally, that they were expected to live up to those standards of quality in their lives after college. Kahn never documented any affection for the updated gargoyles and faux-buttresses he encountered in New Haven. Nevertheless, his subsequent work suggests that the Yale experience began to recast his social idealism from one committed to the "masses," who would be well served by low-cost housing, to one committed to institutions with the vision and the means to become cultural catalysts. An opportunity to express his new direction in built form suddenly appeared at his very doorstep.

FIVE | FRAMING THE MESSAGE

While by 1951, Louis Kahn had a solid portfolio as a creator of low-cost housing, and had designed a small synagogue in Philadelphia as well as several private houses, he had no truly significant buildings to his name. That changed in January when Yale University invited him to design an addition to its art gallery. The assignment came, like his original invitation to teach at Yale, almost by default, but it launched him as an architect who was more than an idealistic academic. The gallery commission was followed by one for a community center near Trenton, New Jersey. It was a minor job by any measure, but it proved to be a design breakthrough, and together with the Yale commission it marked Kahn's emergence not merely as an architect who could build, but as a creative force to be reckoned with. These buildings were crucial testing grounds for his evolving design philosophy, but as he was expanding his reputation as a builder, Kahn was also creating a parallel—and catalytic—role as an educator.

Early in his time at Yale, Kahn developed a reputation among many of his students as a quirky lawgiver with an unorthodox approach to design. As one alumnus observed, he was given to odd utterances, such as "You are doing the wrong thing very carefully" and "I don't like designs in my soup."[1] Another student recalled coming back to the studio in Weir Hall one night and hearing Kahn declare, "When it gets dark enough, it has to be light enough so you can see how dark it is."[2]

Kahn was a sufficiently idiosyncratic teacher to become the inspiration for a character in a novel. *Native Stone,* written by Edward Gilbert and published in 1956, tells the story of three Yale architecture students who go on to assorted adventures in their professional lives. The section on their time at Yale includes this description of an unmistakable Kahn-like member of the faculty: "There he was — Homer Jepson — an almost gnome-like figure encased in in an oxford-gray suit, all three buttons buttoned. Though he always wore an elegant foulard bow tie, it was always indifferently knotted, so that one end hung down, dangled inelegantly. The faintly bulging light blue eyes dominated his small face, the lumpy nose, and always one clump of gray steel-wool hair hung over his furrowed forehead."[3]

Yale's powerful array of faculty talent was steadily enhanced by Kahn's growing reputation. One undergraduate who had been accepted to the architecture programs at both Yale and Penn consulted the Penn dean on his choices, and the dean replied, "Why would you even *consider* turning down Yale?"[4] Once in New Haven, the same student described a typical experience of Kahn's teaching style. In a class that involved circulation patterns in multifamily houses, Kahn ignored the technicalities and explained the goal this way: "When a ball bounces down a step, you don't want a child to run into the road and get hit by a car."[5] Though the lesson was clearly not about square footage, and it's actual meaning was not entirely clear, it nevertheless remained with the student throughout his professional life as a way to explore the human needs of architectural design.

Not all of Kahn's students were impressed by his unorthodox style. According to Ludovica Schniewind, one of only three women in the program at the time, "Kahn did not express himself well; it was difficult to follow him. Many students were disappointed."[6] Another student detected a disturbingly self-serving aspect of Kahn's pedagogical persona. "Lou needed adoration," he remembered. "He coveted our worship, and he played it. At one point, he told us, 'I'm in it for the fame, not the money.' After a visit to the school by Mies [van der Rohe], I saw the vanity and the jealousy." Nevertheless, the same student concluded, "Lou was unbelievably charismatic, he had a glow about him. We loved him."[7]

Kahn's role as a teacher was suddenly amplified in 1951 by the aforementioned commission for an addition to the venerable Beaux-Arts Yale University Art Gallery, designed in 1928 by Egerton Swartwout. The project was not considered a plum. It had been authorized as far back as 1940, but was delayed by the Second World War. An early design by Philip Goodwin, a Yale graduate who had worked with Edward Durell Stone on the innovative 1939 Museum of Modern Art in New York City, had been continually revised but ultimately abandoned due to Goodwin's ill health. The job was then offered to Eero Saarinen, a member of the Yale faculty, who passed it up because his growing office was overburdened with work on the General Motors Technical Center in Warren, Michigan. Philip Johnson, another faculty member who had served as the first director of the Department of Architecture at the Museum of Modern Art, was a plausible candidate proposed by Goodwin, but Saarinen suggested Kahn. As chairman of the department, George Howe, Kahn's former colleague and patron in Philadelphia, was understandably enthusiastic and persuaded Yale's president, A. Whitney Griswold, to support the choice. "The Gallery for Kahn was like being picked from the chorus line to act on Broadway," said Earl Carlin, a student who worked with the architect on the design.[8]

Because the building was to simultaneously house gallery space, administrative offices, and the Department of Architecture, the program was to provide "maximum flexibility," according to the client. More prosaically, in the words of one student who was close to the project, "It was really a parking garage."[9]

With few specifics to guide him, Kahn worked with a local architect, Douglas Orr, and created what was essentially loft space that could be used in a variety of ways and reallocated as necessary. This flexibility was enhanced by Howe's proposal for what came to be called "pogo panels," partitions fitted with spring-loaded shafts at top and bottom that could be moved at will to create individual enclosed areas without compromising the open feeling of the overall space. A more important decision was to cluster the mechanical equipment near the middle of the rectangular structure, providing easy access to the staircase—which Kahn enclosed in a radically sculptural concrete cylinder—as well as the elevators and the air-handling machinery. Although Kahn had yet to codify his decision as a design philosophy, this separation was the beginning of what he later called the distinction between "served" and "servant" spaces, a practice on which he increasingly relied as his career developed.

In addition to the separation of mechanical and open spaces into discrete zones, the second major distinguishing feature of the gallery design was its ceiling. At the time, Anne Tyng, who was an enthusiastic supporter of R. Buckminster Fuller's geodesic theories, exerted a major influence on Kahn's design thinking. At Yale, this took the form of a concrete ceiling slab perforated with tetrahedral openings that would serve as a "space frame," permitting an unusually long span without supporting columns. Tyng was pressing her interest in pure geometry, and the use of this system appealed to her at an almost metaphysical level, symbolizing the confluence of abstraction and function. Kahn seemed more focused on the potential of the system to create a structurally self-supporting concrete space frame that would allow for large spans uninterrupted by columns (and would compensate for the shortage of steel that was a result of the Korean War). A full-scale mock-up survived a test with heavy loads, but engineers for the City of New Haven invoked local building codes that required more conventional support. Reluctantly, Kahn reinforced the slab, compromising its conceptual purity. According to Earl Carlin, the result was "one strong beam; the others are more or less decorative."[10]

The architect was disappointed by the decision, but he was comforted that the openings in the three-foot-thick honeycomb structure could be exploited by threading electrical and air-handling ducts through them. Indeed, as one student involved in the design concluded, "the most interesting idea was the integration of structure and mechanical, not the geodesic stuff."[11] Likely more important to the architect than structural self-sufficiency or even mechanical convenience was the look of the slab from below. Its powerful three-dimensional alternation of light and shadow created a visual statement that has been the signature of the building ever since (see color plate 3 and the cover of this volume). This would not be the last time Kahn cloaked his fondness for theatrical effects with the air of practicality.

The commission that had languished for so long before Kahn's appointment became an instant critical success. The critic Frederick Gutheim commented on the building's November 1953 completion in the *New York Herald Tribune,* observing that "Yale University's new Art building, designed by Louis Kahn of Philadelphia, strikes me as the outstanding academic building thus far produced by the modern movement in architecture."[12] Gutheim went on to declare that "a bold and highly original designer of world rank has established himself with this building."

The impact of the Yale gallery helped secure Kahn another commission, this one for a Jewish community center near Trenton, New Jersey, in February 1955. Although the bathhouse that Kahn designed was only a fragment of a larger, unexecuted plan, it has since become one of the classics of late modern architecture. Again working with Anne Tyng, Kahn created four hollow pavilions arranged like a plus sign. These were topped by shallow pyramidal roofs and contained changing rooms for bathers, flanking a central open space that served as both an open-air common room and a crossroads for the club's other users. What most distinguished the design was the combination of elemental geometry and pure functionality. But it was in no way a cold or unsympathetic building. On the contrary, by lifting the roof slightly off the pavilions at all four corners, Kahn lightened the sense of mass while providing an ample supply of natural light. The Trenton Bath House marked a masterful balance of delicacy and solidity, while evoking echoes of a historical architectural form that might be traced to the fascination Kahn developed for Roman ruins on his trip to that city in 1950–51.

With his credentials as a designer growing, Kahn was offered the chairmanship of the Yale department, but turned it down. Vincent Scully recalled telephoning Kahn and pleading with him: "I said, 'You're the greatest teacher in the world, but you probably won't design many buildings. Why won't you take it?' He said: 'I'm going to design more buildings than anybody else in the United States,' and he slammed down the phone. Then he called me back and said he was sorry."[13] Kahn's decision no doubt reflected his growing professional confidence; his Philadelphia practice was picking up. But he had also developed a dislike for the man who would become chair in 1957, a Harvard-trained architect named Paul Rudolph. Although Kahn had been disappointed awaiting an invitation to design another building at

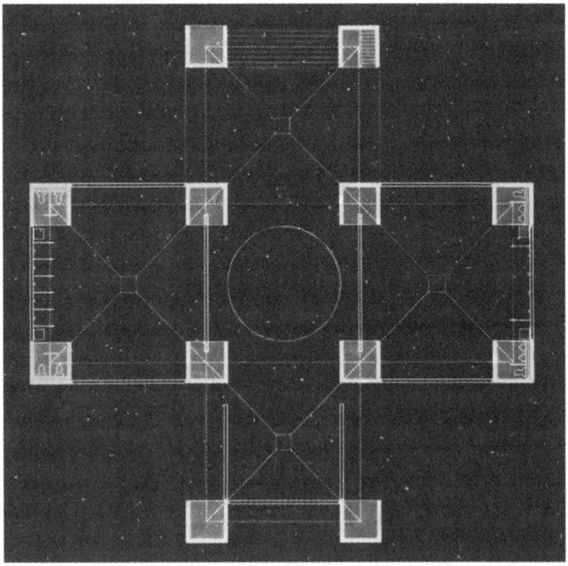

FIGURE 19. Floor plan of the Trenton Bath House. (Louis I. Kahn Collection, University of Pennsylvania and Pennsylvania Historical and Museum Commission)

FIGURE 20. The Trenton Bath House as built (1955). (Louis I. Kahn Collection, University of Pennsylvania and Pennsylvania Historical and Museum Commission)

FIGURE 21. Kahn with his colleague Anne Tyng. (Anne Griswold Tyng Collection, The Architectural Archives, University of Pennsylvania)

Yale, an additional reason for his rebuffs of the university's repeated appeals may have been the expectation that he would have to serve on the jury for one of Rudolph's studio assignments, for a "roadside frozen custard stand."[14]

After brief intervals teaching part-time at MIT and Princeton, Kahn found his way back to Philadelphia. The individual primarily responsible for his move was G. Holmes Perkins, who had until recently been teaching at the GSD. Having hoped but failed to succeed Gropius at Harvard, Perkins transferred in 1951 to Penn, where he set out to reenergize a program that

FIGURE 22. Kahn in his Master Class at the University of Pennsylvania. (James F. Williamson Collection, The Architectural Archives, University of Pennsylvania)

had slipped in stature behind the GSD and Yale. A key element in his strategy was Louis I. Kahn, whom he had known during the 1940s through the American Society of Planners and Architects, and to whom he made an offer in 1955. Kahn accepted, and for five years he taught a variety of courses to advanced Penn students. In 1960 Perkins invited him to conduct a series of Master Classes for students who already had their first professional degrees. In the world of architectural education, Kahn's class would become known as "the most famous course in the USA."[15]

Unlike Yale, where he had arrived from Philadelphia as a relative neophyte in an institution brimming with major talents and personalities, Penn gave the more seasoned Kahn an opportunity to create an environment entirely his own. In doing so, he fashioned what struck some students as a sort of architectural royal court, whose members he was free to appoint. Among them was Norman Rice, his fellow Penn architecture graduate who had worked for Le Corbusier, as well as Robert LeRicolais, a French-born engineer, and Carles Vallhonrat, an elegant but personally frosty Spanish architect. They were joined by August Komendant, a fellow Estonian who had been trained as an engineer in Germany and had developed his expert knowledge of concrete by studying Nazi submarine pens in France before emigrating to the United States. Finally, there was a mysterious figure named Gabor Antala Szalontay, a Hungarian with a murky professional history who seemed to function as Kahn's resident muse, drifting into studio sessions and making cryptic observations that only Kahn seemed to appreciate. Kahn explained Gabor's role as "a man in my office who doesn't do any work. But I gladly pay him because he helps me think."[16]

Thinking was what Kahn evidently hoped to stimulate in his students. Indeed, creativity took precedence over technical learning, as the four-hundred-odd students who passed through his classes remembered with mixed emotions. According to James Williamson, a student in the Master Class, "no time was spent on teaching practical professional skills such as compliance with the requirements of a program, graphic presentation techniques or construction documentation, since acceptance into the program was based on demonstrated ability to do those things already."[17]

Many of Kahn's Penn students, like those at Yale, were enthralled by his teaching. According to Max A. Robinson, a student in the Master Class of 1964, "his elaborations upon the notions of silence, light, wonder, joy, knowledge, realizations, singularities, the measurable and the Unmeasurable [*sic*] offered insights into the depth and extent of his ideas and presented us with a gauge by which we could measure our own attempts."[18] Some students were so captivated by their teacher's words that they even took in stride Kahn's habit of napping in class while still seated in his chair.[19] A few even began to imitate their teacher's dress, affecting black bow ties, and his high-pitched voice.[20]

In conducting his Master Class, Kahn proved more rambling in language than he'd been at Yale. Even his most worshipful students could find the presentations hard to handle. As Charles Dagit recalled, "Because Lou spent hours talking about architecture, some of which we understood but a great deal of which went over us, it frequently meant for me a headache of monumental proportions after listening intently for eight hours or so to try to understand his prodigious mind."[21] Kahn's teaching colleague August Komendant brought an engineer's impatience to some of Kahn's pronouncements, noting that "he was not able to teach design in a practical sense." As evidence, he cited a typical class observation by the "master" in his memoir: "Knowledge is in man because he is made out of nature. The stuff is it. It is answerable to all universal laws."[22] Komendant forgave such wooliness because, as he put it, Kahn "was superb for inspiring and criticizing a design."[23] Vincent Scully, who had been such a supporter of Kahn's at Yale, was not so kind, eventually finding his former colleague trying. "He used words as a smokescreen," Scully observed. "It began to overtake him. It was embarrassing."[24] But according to his elder daughter, Kahn talked not so much to make a point as to explore concepts and solutions that were as yet unclear to him. "Teaching was his way of connecting and working out ideas," she said.

While Kahn was considered a cult leader in the eyes of some skeptics, he was not interested in creating clones. Sue Ann Kahn concedes that her father could be hard on students who did not make a sufficient effort in his eyes. "He was tough-minded" she recalls, "but he was never unkind. He was looking for something better rather than tearing something down. He was trying to encourage students to be creative on their own, not to copy anyone else, including himself."[25] According to James Williamson, Kahn "was encouraging them to reject their prior learning and to trust their intuition as more powerful than their analytical capacity."[26]

For all his charisma and apparent concern for their creative potential, Kahn struck many students as emotionally distant, even cold. As one of his Penn students observed, "he seemed to discourage personal relationships with his students, and my main impression of his personality was its combination of strength and remoteness."[27] His students served more as audiences than individuals, and on occasion he could be harsh. In his memoir, Dagit reports an incident when Kahn, having examined a student presentation, announced: "This building is a turd on the landscape. Whose is it?"[28]

The class often included problems Kahn was working on in his practice, among them a number of private houses. Over the course of his career, Kahn designed numerous residences, but completed only nine, all in the Philadelphia area. Although the finished projects were limited in number, the domestic works served as laboratories for later and more ambitious commissions. According to William Whitaker, curator of the architectural archives at the University of Pennsylvania and coauthor of a monograph on Kahn's houses, "they spoke, often before his larger commissions did, to many of the issues that stirred him as an architect." The domestic designs were "every bit as compelling for him, and as pivotal for his work, as the design of his other buildings."[29] Central to the house designs were natural materials, especially wood and local stone, and the manipulation of natural light.

In contrast to many modernist domestic designs of the period, which emphasized free-flowing open spaces, clean lines, and large expanses of glass, Kahn's houses reflected a concern for spatial variety and physical texture. All of the houses are characterized by a range of intimate spaces, often including fireplaces with inglenooks to encourage small gatherings and conversation. Where more orthodox contemporary designs might be characterized by smooth surfaces, modular geometry, and machined finishes, Kahn's domestic buildings, most notably the Esherick (see color plate 4) and Fisher houses, were marked by a rich combination of rough masonry, spatial surprises, and natural wood.

According to Sue Ann Kahn, her father had once described an ideal vision of a home as a place where, "if an outsider were looking in . . . he could see a woman cooking over a stove, a happy family with the light glowing."[30] Ironically, Kahn's own home life was anything but ideal. Indeed, his relationship with Anne Tyng had put heavy strains on Kahn's marriage to Esther, with whom he was still living in her parents' house while he tended to Anne's daughter on the sly. Those strains only increased as Kahn moved on from Tyng to other romantic liaisons. Beyond that, there was likely some level of frustration at dealing with the inevitable small-scale issues involved in working with clients on their personal spaces. Kahn at this point in his career was clearly ready for more ambitious undertakings.

If Kahn had begun to consolidate his search for an architectural philosophy in his early teaching at Yale and his seminal trip to Rome, he refined it through the actual construction of the Yale Art Gallery addition and the Trenton Bath House. The expansion of his teaching role through the Master Class at Penn—combined with the steady development of his ideas about space, materials, and light in the design of his private houses—had prepared him for something more. Kahn had never faltered in the commitment he had developed as a young man that architecture could create a better world. The next step would combine all these influences with what he had begun to appreciate at Yale about architecture's potential for improving society through powerful institutions.

He did not have far to look. In 1957, his alma mater offered him a major commission on the Penn campus. Although ultimately flawed in many respects, the Alfred Newton Richards Medical Research Building moved Kahn beyond the mere framing of his abstract architectural message to delivering it in built form on the world stage.

SIX | LESSONS IN LEARNING

One of Louis Kahn's most repeated—and accessible—pronouncements was about how the concept of a school was born. It all started, he told any number of audiences over the years, "with a man under a tree." The man, said Kahn, "did not know he was a teacher, and those who listened to him did not consider themselves pupils or students. They were just there, and they liked the experience of being in the presence of one who had a realization—a sense of order."[1] The image is at once simple and complex. The knowledgeable person is recognized by those eager to learn. But how did the teacher realize he had something to offer that the others would value? And how did the listeners know that the person speaking had anything important to say?

By the time Kahn received the commission for the Alfred Newton Richards Medical Research Building at the University of Pennsylvania in February 1957, he was already a legendary teacher; as his fame spread, his lectures were increasingly attended by people outside the architecture school who considered them almost as theatrical events. Nevertheless, Kahn had limited experience in building beyond the relatively small scale of the Yale University Art Gallery addition, his few residences, a small synagogue, a humble facility for the American Federation of Labor in Philadelphia, and the Trenton Bath House. A fair amount of his reputation in the architectural community rested on some wildly speculative schemes for the redevelopment of downtown Philadelphia. The teacher had a great deal to learn.

At the time, the Penn campus had an eclectic collection of buildings. The university had moved in 1872 from its former location in central Philadelphia to a site on the edge of the city. It had a masterful 1890s mock-Tudor dormitory complex designed by the accomplished eclectic firm of Cope and Stewardson, and a spectacular 1890 library by the flamboyantly unorthodox architect Frank Furness, which housed the studio where Kahn taught his Master Class. But Penn had none of the serene symmetry of Thomas Jefferson's grounds for the University of Virginia, the urban anchoring of Harvard Yard, or the stylistic consistency of the neo-Gothic architecture that James Gamble Rogers had provided for Yale. Penn was ripe for a significant modern landmark, and Kahn was poised to expand his commitment to social betterment through another powerful institution.

Kahn's opportunity came via G. Holmes Perkins, who as head of Penn's School of Fine Arts had recruited him from Yale and was evidently satisfied that Kahn was now sufficiently well established to make a physical mark on Penn.

The commission for the Richards Medical Research Building posed a major problem: Kahn had had no experience in the design of laboratories or any other medical facilities. In his memoir, *18 Years With Architect Louis I. Kahn,* the engineer August Komendant acknowledged the situation by recalling Kahn's statement to him: "Architecture has to provide useful spaces, but at least one has to know what these spaces are for and how they are related to each other."[2]

Another concern—one which Kahn successfully avoided in all his subsequent important buildings—was the absence of an authoritative individual who could provide overall guidance on the goals of the building. The Richards building was to be used jointly by Penn's departments of surgery, physiology, microbiology, botany, and zoology, among others. The head of each department had specific requirements, but there was no coordination.

FIGURE 23. The Richards Medical Research Building at the University of Pennsylvania under construction, showing its innovative structural system. (August Komendant Collection, The Architectural Archives, University of Pennsylvania)

"The client," remembered G. Holmes Perkins many years later with obvious regret, "was a committee."[3]

Without firm or consistent guidance, Kahn designed the building as he imagined scientists would want it to be, but he assumed that they would work best the way architects did—in studios. According to Komendant, "the studio image, to start with, was very attractive and [Kahn] thought it would provide the best environment also for scientific work."[4] Proceeding from that image, Kahn designed the project as a cluster of four eight-story towers arranged like the wings of a pinwheel, one housing mechanical equipment and space for the animals that would be used in experiments, and the other three devoted to laboratory facilities. Two additional towers for biology were later added. The organization recalls and advances the separation of "served" and "servant" spaces that the architect had used horizontally at the Yale gallery, but extends the approach vertically.

The visual impact of the Richards composition is striking. The window-

FIGURE 24. For some critics, the completed Richards building evoked historical precedents that suggested a path beyond modernism. (©Richard Lautman Photography, National Building Museum)

less brick columns create a sense of thrusting verticality and support, while the laboratory floors provide the composition with a balanced horizontality, their glazed facades making a pleasing contrast with the rough texture of the masonry.

When it opened, in 1961, Richards was a critical sensation, covered in more than two hundred publications in the United States and abroad, and the subject of a one-building show at New York's Museum of Modern Art. One writer later declared that, "In its functionalism, response to program, honesty in use of materials, and use of glass, the building is a culmination of modern architecture. At the same time it transcends modern architecture and becomes something new."[5] Vincent Scully, regardless of his growing reservations about Kahn's verbosity as a teacher, speculated that the architect had found a solution to one of modernism's most serious shortcomings: its abandonment of architectural history. In his 1962 monograph, Scully described the Richards building as "reminiscent surely of San Gimignano and Siena."[6] On the surface, the connection made sense. Kahn had visited both Italian hill towns during his stay at the American Academy in Rome, and there is an undeniable visual similarity between the forms of the towers in Italy and Philadelphia. But Kahn vigorously dismissed the connection, insisting that Richards was an original conception generated by the program and the cramped site. Never one to concede artistic influence, he may have overstated his position. In any case, Scully's interpretation had a fundamental impact on American architects.

Ever since Ludwig Mies van der Rohe had finished his elegantly austere Seagram Building in New York City, architects such as Edward Durell Stone, Eero Saarinen, and Philip Johnson had been searching for ways to reintroduce visual and emotional appeal in architecture. The very suggestion that Kahn had drawn on medieval sources suddenly afforded permission to revisit historical precedents, something that had been proscribed by orthodox modernism.

One of the most ringing endorsements of Richards came from the architectural historian William Jordy. In a thorough analysis of its importance, he concluded that "Kahn's building is real in its tangibility; real in materials and structure; ostensibly, if not literally, real in the inevitability with which the composition unfolds from a functional conception; hence real in its scorn of superficial beauty. If 'beautiful' at all, it is so as a dogmatic manifestation of character."[7]

Not all the response to Richards was so positive. Reyner Banham, an English critic, was especially harsh; in withering prose, he pointed out the conflict between the building's apparent message of structure and mass and its manipulation of form for visual effect.[8] The most obvious example was the contrast between the fully enclosed mini-towers, which can be read as solid supports for the laboratory floors but actually contain exhaust ducts, and those towers that housed stairs but were open at the top, revealing their hollow-core construction and their very divergent function. In both cases, an architectural element appears to be doing one thing while in fact it is doing another, a fundamental betrayal of modernist doctrine that structure be expressed honestly. Banham's criticisms recalled the debate over the Yale Art Gallery floor slab, which in the end proved its worth more as stage set than as structure. But those complaints seemed almost puritanical when measured against the Richards building's formidable aesthetic impact. It was nothing less than a declaration that glass-and-steel modernism had finally succumbed to a renewed appetite for visual interest, symbolism, and historical association.

More damning than the stylistic criticisms were the judgments of the users. Scientists complained of crowding, inadequate storage space, excessive noise that traveled across the open ceilings, and sunlight that flooded their labs so pervasively that many occupants draped the windows with metal foil. Komendant defended his architect: "All these deficiencies may be true," he wrote in his memoir, "but blaming Kahn for them is unjustified. Kahn, having no experience of his own for laboratory design, only carried out what the doctors asked and wanted."[9] According to John MacAllister, who worked on the building in Kahn's office, many of the shortcomings could be attributed to "value engineering," the practice of removing elements of a design or reducing the quality of materials in order to save money late in the process; "I think the only way one could fault Kahn was that he allowed these changes so the design could be saved,"[10] he observed. Among the changes were the substitution of inferior glass for the type originally specified, which would likely have eliminated the problem of

FIGURE 25. Kahn's fellow Estonian and essential engineer, August Komendant. (August Komendant Collection, The Architectural Archives, University of Pennsylvania)

sun glare in the laboratories. Whatever the ultimate responsibility for the functional shortcomings of Richards, the university was sufficiently concerned that it removed Kahn from principal involvement in the construction of the biology buildings he had designed for the adjacent site. More painful was Penn's decision not to consider Kahn for any future projects on the campus, including a building for the fine arts, which he claimed to have been promised.[11]

These problems did not extend to the building's engineering. Indeed, by working with Komendant, Kahn had developed a new appreciation of the potential of prestressed concrete, a material that made the long spans of the Richards laboratories possible. Kahn's work with the material was not limited to its structural properties. In the enclosed staircase of the Yale Art Gallery, Kahn had left the marks of the wooden forms on the concrete, realizing their potential as a sort of decoration that had been shunned by many architects devoted to the finished surfaces of steel, glass and stucco. At Richards, the concrete surfaces were also left unfinished, not so much for visual appeal but to communicate the way in which the members were formed.

Happily for Kahn, an opportunity soon presented itself that enabled him to benefit from the lessons of Richards, which involved far more than architecture and engineering. Kahn for the first time encountered the condition that would animate all of his subsequent successful buildings: a close personal relationship with a powerful client. His days of working with committees were behind him.

Jonas Salk, who had become world-famous for his work on developing a vaccine to prevent polio, had decided to build a research center, and in 1959 was advised to consult with Kahn on how to select an architect, as Kahn was the most prominent designer working on something close to what Salk was after. After a visit to Kahn's office and a tour of the Richards building, Salk was sufficiently impressed by the architect and his work to cut his search short and hire the Philadelphian. "It was love at first sight," he recalled.[12] Salk described Kahn as "a tiny, whimsical man who happened by chance to have the vision of an artist, the understanding of a philosopher, the knowledge of a metaphysician, and the reason of a logician . . . We understood each other completely."[13]

There was more than architecture to their connection. Like Kahn, Salk was from an eastern European Jewish family that had immigrated to the United States. Like Kahn, he had benefited from excellent public schooling, in Salk's case in New York City. And like Kahn, Salk had a romantic's vision: in his case, of what science could do for mankind. Trained as a medical doctor, Salk went on to do research in virology. Having had spectacular success in developing his polio vaccine, and having attracted substantial financial backing as a result, Salk hoped to bring the world's leading scientific and cultural thinkers together as fellows in search of catalytic solutions to the rest of the world's problems, whether scientific or more wide-ranging. The purpose of what became the Salk Institute for Biological Studies, as he recalled in 1984, "was to serve and to celebrate the process of creativity; to form a crucible for creativity not only in the life sciences, but in the arts, the humanities and in philosophy. It was to be a place that would be concerned with evolving human values and human knowledge."[14] Kahn might well have described his ambitions for the institute in identical terms.

The site Salk chose for the institution that would house these efforts covered twenty-seven acres on a dramatic cliff overlooking the Pacific near La Jolla called Torrey Pines Mesa. After discarding an earlier and larger scheme, Salk and Kahn (see color plate 5) settled on two parallel six-story

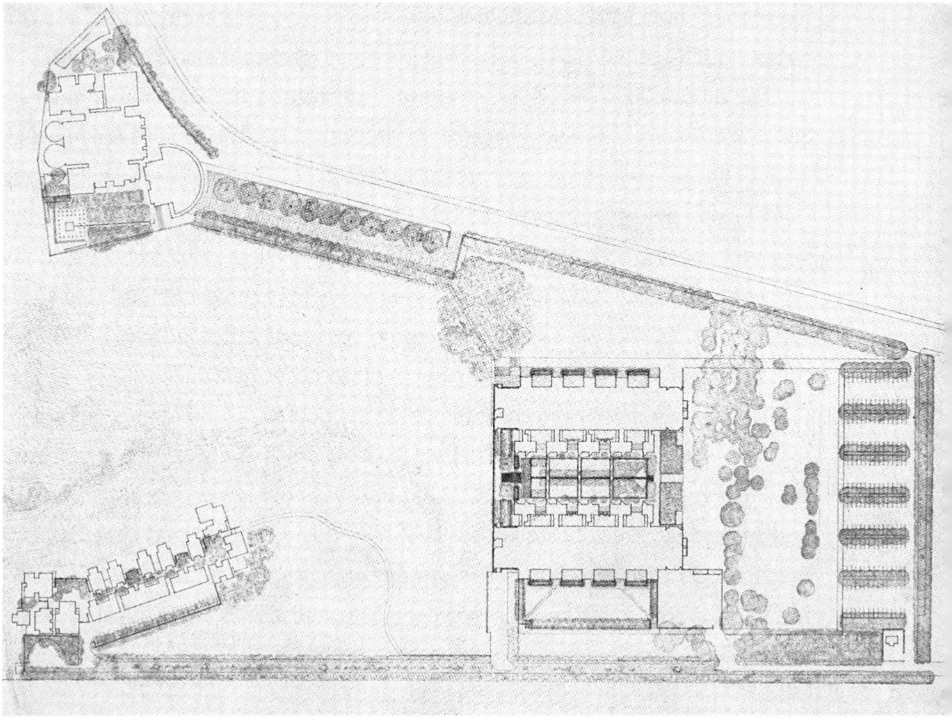

FIGURE 26. Site plan for the Salk Institute for Biological Studies showing the unbuilt meeting house at upper left. (Louis I. Kahn Collection, University of Pennsylvania and Pennsylvania Historical and Museum Commission)

buildings facing each other across a courtyard that was open at both ends: one facing inland, the other toward the sea. The facades of the main buildings were punctuated with rows of four-story structures intended as individual studies for the institute fellows, each angled outward to provide a view of the ocean. According to John MacAllister, who oversaw the work at Salk, it was conceived of "as at once an institution and a village. Just as the professors had their pavilions on the Lawn at the University of Virginia, the Salk fellows had their studies: places that were at once part of, but apart from, the whole."[15] Down the center of the plaza was a narrow channel for water, which spilled into a reflecting pool and a basin at the Pacific end.

The open plaza, paved in travertine and split by the water channel, has become the iconic public image of the institute, but the functional success of the complex was more important to its users. Sensitive to criticism that the laboratories at Richards had been cramped, here Kahn designed unobstructed open spaces that could be configured as the researchers saw fit. As one scientist observed, "my lab flows into the lab next to me and that's the valuable thing. The sparks fly at the boundaries of different areas of scientific research. People are always running into other people."[16]

The open spaces owed their flexibility to August Komendant's engineering. The main features were thirteen Vierendeel trusses, structural beams nine feet high and sixty-five feet long that supported the laboratory floors and were deep enough to allow virtually all the mechanical functions to be threaded through them. The system was in essence an expanded and improved version of the space-frame Kahn had used at the Yale Art Gallery, and by creating uninterrupted spaces eliminated the main complaint lodged by researchers about Richards.

The basic material of the complex was concrete, but it was treated with extraordinary sensitivity under the direction of Fred Langford, one of Kahn's employees. The forms into which the concrete was poured were made of polyurethane-coated plywood which, when removed, left a surface almost as smooth as polished stone. Rather than concealing the joints between the concrete panels, Kahn emphasized them by creating V-shaped recesses, relieving what might have been an oppressively uniform surface and adding a sense of scale to the overall composition. The recesses where the ends of the metal tie-rods holding the forms together normally would have been patched, but Kahn chose to accentuate them with lead plugs, creating a sort of visual punctuation that compensated for the lack of other detail. Complementing the concrete were inset panels of teak wood that aged in the sea air to a rich brownish gray (see color plate 6). Kahn had explored the juxtaposition of concrete and wood—hard and soft—in several of his private house commissions, but now it would become a characteristic of most of his future designs.

For all of its success as a facility for science, the institute fell short of the ambitious vision shared by Salk and Kahn as a place for more wide-ranging inquiry. The individual studies facing the Pacific had been intended as places of intellectual contemplation and creativity, but the fellows generally preferred mingling with each other in the laboratories, and in many cases the spaces ended up serving as little more than storage units. More disappointing was the shortfall of funds to complete the meeting house, a building that would have been located a short distance from the main complex, intended to provide a refuge from the day-to-day activities in the labs, with meeting rooms, a library, and an auditorium arranged around a central courtyard. Both the architect and the client had envisioned a gathering place that would provide a physical expression of their belief in the interdisciplinary nature of knowledge. By the time the main buildings were complete, however, the money had run out. Its loss was perhaps the greatest disappointment for both of the Salk Institute's creators.

The loss was offset in some measure by what some might have considered a minor commission. Although the architect was already involved in two projects on the Indian subcontinent—the Indian Institute of Management in Ahmedabad and the government center for East Pakistan (later Bangladesh) in Dhaka—as well as a Unitarian church in Rochester New York, he took on a relatively small assignment much closer to home. At the time, one of Jonas Salk's sons, Peter, was a student at Phillips Exeter Academy, an independent boarding school in southern New Hampshire, which had outgrown its library, a 1912 Beaux-Arts building designed by Ralph Adams Cram. The architect of many of Exeter's brick dormitories, Cram had modeled his library on an English manor house, but it no longer suited the academy's needs. Peter suggested to the school's librarian, Rodney Armstrong (who had been his faculty adviser), that he consider Kahn for the commission. The library building committee interviewed several of the country's leading architects, including Edward Larrabee Barnes, Philip Johnson, I. M. Pei, Paul Rudolph, Eero Saarinen, and Edward Durell Stone, but Kahn won out, principally because, as at Salk, the fit between architect and commission was far more than a matter of professional qualifications. According to the colorful assessment of one member of the selection committee, Kahn "ought to find appealing the chance to build for such young as we see here, for whom the tough and the beautiful are both familiar aspects of the deep life they seek."[17]

Phillips Exeter Academy was founded in 1781 with a purpose significantly different from that of many later American boarding schools. Rather than serving as a finishing school for the wealthy as they headed to elite colleges, Exeter was to prepare students for the "great end and real business of living." It was dedicated to offering superior education to the humble as well as the powerful, and according to its charter, Exeter's mission was "educating youth from every quarter . . . well considering that goodness without knowledge is weak and feeble, yet knowledge without goodness is dangerous, and that both united form the noblest of character, and lay the surest foundation of usefulness to mankind."[18] Indeed, the motto of the school, *Finis Origine Pendet,* Latin for "The End Depends on the Beginning," signaled its concern for character as well as accomplishment. It was also uncannily close to one of Kahn's favorite aphorisms: "What will be has always been."[19]

As with the Salk Institute, the Exeter connection between architect and client was both intimate and powerful. The commission called for "a laboratory for research and experimentation, a quiet retreat for study, reading and reflection, the intellectual center of the community." Kahn frequently insisted that he was not a reader, but that he nevertheless revered books, and his design reflected that reverence with singular impact. According to Rodney Armstrong, a navy veteran of the Second World War who shepherded the project to completion, "Libraries were an ideal to Kahn. He looked at our program, which was vague, and caught the spirit of what we wanted."[20]

The design of the building is deceptively simple. From the outside, it appears to be little more than a symmetrical brick cube (see color plate 7), which rises nearly four stories at the center of the Exeter campus. Like the Yale Art Gallery and the Richards Laboratories, the entrance is muted, hidden in the enclosed arcade that encloses the first floor. But at the corners, Kahn pulled the facades back to reveal their thinness as screens, lightening the mass of the cube. To soften the potentially harsh impact of the brick, he inserted panels of teak beneath the windows, as he had at the Salk Institute.

The exterior of the Exeter library belies the drama that awaits inside. A double staircase leads up from the ground floor and virtually explodes onto an atrium that extends to the top of the building. The atrium is surrounded on all sides by a zone of book stacks, which is in turn bordered by a ring of study carrels with windows to the outside (see color plate 8). Using concrete to spectacular effect, Kahn cut enormous circular openings in the walls of the atrium, providing views across the open space through the stacks to the windows. In doing so, he created a constantly changing vista of activity: students circulating around the atrium had a view of the traffic at the circulation desk below, but could also see across to the activity in the book stacks and through to the carrels beyond. While Kahn never admitted to a connection, he might have been invoking memories of the bustling life of the streets in Philadelphia's Northern Liberties of his childhood, or the urban vitality of the Italian hill towns he had visited while in Rome. In any case, the Exeter library creates a uniquely dynamic interplay of heavy masonry forms and delicate human interaction.

Amplifying the devices he had developed at Salk to create visual interest (the lead plugs for the tie-rod ends, the V-shaped joints between the concrete panels), Kahn called out the connections between expanses of con-

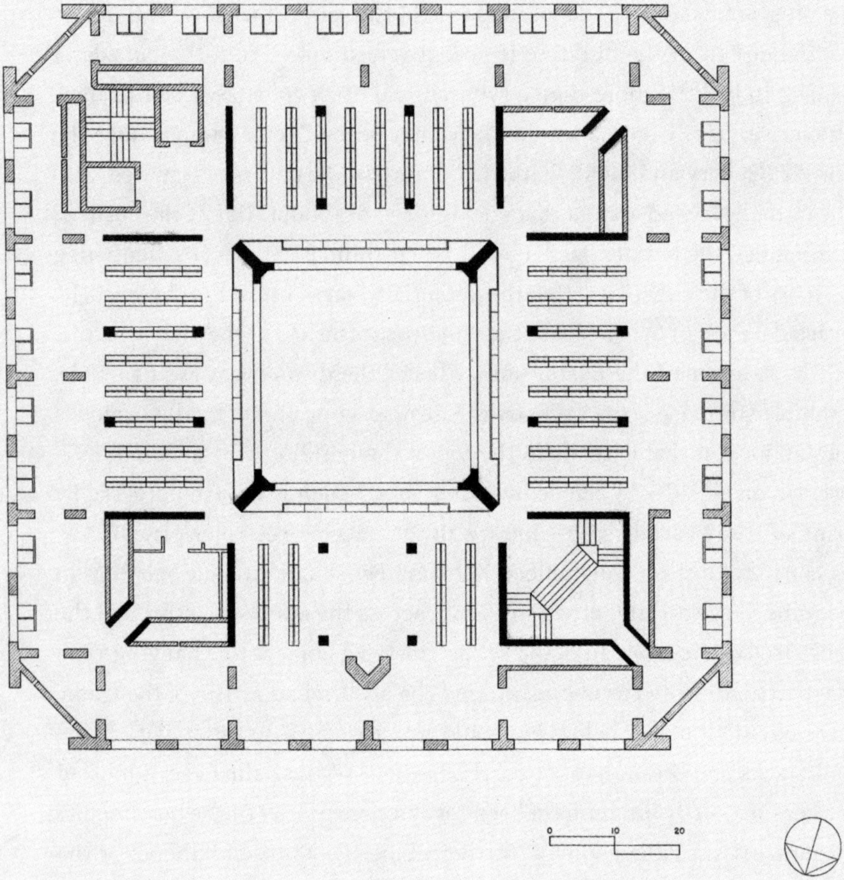

FIGURE 27. Exeter floor plan, showing the ring of book stacks centered on the atrium. (Louis I. Kahn Collection, University of Pennsylvania and Pennsylvania Historical and Museum Commission)

crete at Exeter in a way that vividly, if unnecessarily, highlights the way the members are assembled. The effect is such that a child could understand the structure of the building, while appreciating the play of the surfaces as a visual composition. As on the brick exterior, the chill of the interior concrete is warmed by facing the balconies with wood—in this case, white oak. When it was dedicated in 1972, Kahn's building was celebrated as the world's largest secondary-school library.[21] But its impact went far beyond the 160,000 volumes it housed. The design was considered by many to be an almost perfect architectural embodiment of the idea of education: a place that encouraged learning by creating a sense of wonder at the importance of books.

The excitement over the library was tempered by disappointment with the dining hall that Kahn designed for a site adjacent to the larger building. The request for the facility was received after the library design was underway, in June of 1966, and Kahn evidently invested less creativity in the project. But it was hardly the stepchild to the library it was later made out to be. In a letter to the Exeter principal after receiving the added commission, Kahn commented, in his characteristically quirky prose, "I appreciate the opportunity which both buildings, in wake of each other, give me to find the architectural order strong and resourceful to express each in its own use, yet architecturally in sympathy with each other."[22] An added but crucially important aspect of the dining hall complex was that it provided space for mechanical systems that otherwise would have been housed in the library, which would have reduced square footage for books and study.

A major problem posed by the library was the quality of the construction, something that would plague the school for years and require more than $7 million in renovations. A telling example was the windows, which were inserted directly against the brick, without the normal flashing that would have kept out rain and snow. "Caulking was not enough," observed an Exeter maintenance official who had to deal with the problem.[23] Responsibility was ultimately assigned to the contractors, but the problems recalled August Komendant's observations that Kahn's primary focus was on the message of a building, rather than the making of it.

Complaints also persisted about the absence of a clear entrance to the building. In fact, a plan for a forecourt and associated landscaping had been developed by a member of Kahn's staff, Harriet Pattison, whose arrangement would have created a welcome locator for the hidden front door. (In addition to her work on the library, Pattison had succeeded Anne Tyng as Kahn's lover, and in 1962 bore him a son, Nathaniel. Like the relationship with Tyng, this one was kept quiet.) Pattison's schematics for the building were canceled to save money, leaving the library's users to solve the mystery of how to get in.

The failure to complete the Salk meeting house had been a setback for Kahn's idealistic dedication to the pursuit of ways to make the world a better place through institutions. The Exeter library, a four-story building for a New England boarding school, allowed him to resolve the missteps he had made at Richards in designing for users with whom he was unfamiliar; the idea of a sanctuary for learning was central to his understanding of architecture's potential. Not surprisingly, the building had an impact far beyond its modest size and location. Writing in the *New York Times,* Ada Louise Huxtable, the country's most prominent architectural critic at the time, declared that "the new building exemplified much that has made Kahn the dean of American architects."[24] In designing it, Kahn had learned as much as he taught.

SEVEN | ART FOR ART'S SAKE

Louis Kahn might never have designed a building if it had not been for the architectural history course he took as a schoolboy under William F. Gray in Philadelphia. Indeed, Kahn had originally hoped to be an artist, and his talent in drawing and painting surely qualified him for that role. Having become an architect, however, Kahn in his later years was able to serve his first passion with supreme effect through his second. Between 1966 and his death in 1974, Kahn was able to explore the housing of works of art in two dramatically different environments for two dramatically different collections. The results are among the finest museum structures anywhere. If social uplift had been Kahn's motivation from his earliest days as an architect, his engagement as a mature practitioner with major institutions did as much for art as it did for society at large.

Kahn's experience designing the addition to the Yale University Art Gallery had allowed him to indulge his devotion to art only up to a point. The program there had called for increased exhibition space for the university's growing collection, but it had also specified "maximum flexibility" for teaching and administrative spaces.

The architect had his first unadulterated commission for an art museum in Fort Worth, Texas. The building had its beginnings under Kay Kimbell, an entrepreneur who had grown wealthy in oil, real estate, grain, and retailing, and who in the 1930s, after purchasing his first paintings, established the Kimbell Art Foundation. When Kimbell died in 1964, he and his wife left their collection of approximately 360 works of art—ranging from ivories and jades to British and French old masters from the eighteenth and nineteenth centuries—and most of their fortune to the foundation to create a public art museum.

Two years later, the foundation appointed Richard Fargo Brown as the museum's first director, charging him to "form collections of the highest aesthetic quality, derived from any and all periods in man's history, and in any medium or style."[1] Brown had been a graduate student in art history at Harvard's Fogg Art Museum, where he concentrated on research in vision and color theory, writing a dissertation on Camille Pissarro, and later became a curator at the Frick Collection in New York City. Most recently, Brown had served as director of the Los Angeles County Art Museum. Now he set about searching for an architect to create a museum in Fort Worth to rival the ones he already knew so well.

A product of the East Coast academic establishment, Brown faced a familiar concern about cultural institutions in Texas: While they might be well funded, they were not widely considered among the nation's best. Whether prompted by the region's sense of cultural insecurity, or simply by a desire to do the right thing, Brown drew up a list of architects that included many of the leading names in the profession. It was an unusually eclectic selection. One candidate was Max Abramovitz, a New York architect known for his work on the United Nations headquarters and numerous commercial high-rises. Another was Marcel Breuer, the Bauhaus alumnus who was at work on the Whitney Museum in New York in a distinctive manner that emphasized massive concrete forms. There was Pier Luigi Nervi, an Italian architect known for innovative engineering, and Ludwig Mies van der Rohe, the German master of glass and steel best known for the Seagram Building on New York's Park Avenue.

The site for the Kimbell extended over nine-and-a-half acres near Philip Johnson's 1960 Amon Carter Museum of Western Art, which celebrated such American artists as Frederick Remington. In his description of the program for the Kimbell, Brown had written that he wanted the building to serve members of the public, rather than just connoisseurs and specialists, and that "their total experience of a visit to the museum should be one of warmth, mellowness, and even elegance."[2] No doubt Mies, even in his eighties, would have delivered elegance, but neither he nor the other leading contenders could claim warmth or mellowness as major characteristics of their work. Kahn was awarded the commission on October 5, 1966.

At the time, Kahn's Philadelphia office was all but overwhelmed. The Exeter library was still under construction. Kahn was working on designs for a Unitarian church in Rochester, New York; a performing arts center in Fort Wayne, Indiana; and a factory for the Olivetti-Underwood typewriter company in Harrisburg, Pennsylvania. In addition, he was traveling to India for work on the Indian Institute of Management in Ahmedabad, and to East Pakistan to oversee the early stages of the government center in Dhaka.

Unlike the amorphous program at Yale, the Kimbell's plan called for the display of a highly varied but limited collection. Among the most prominent objects were paintings of the late Renaissance and Baroque periods. Sensitive to the fragility of these works, and with his expertise in vision science and color theory, Brown insisted that "natural light should play a vital part in illumination"[3] of the building, acutely aware of the harm that an excess of natural light could inflict. The solution called on the architect's most creative resources.

Discussing the choice of the forms for Kimbell, Kahn observed somewhat cryptically: "My mind is full of Roman greatness and the vault so etched itself in my mind that, though I can not employ it, it's there always ready, and the vault seems to be the best."[4] What emerged was a symmetrical single-story complex of sixteen repeated forms. These had curved roofs and were arranged in three groups with six set side by side at either end and four in the middle; four of each group of six were devoted to the museum galleries and offices, and two were covered porches flanking the entrance (see color plate 9). The primary material was cast-in-place, post-tensioned reinforced concrete. The program statement developed by Brown asserted that "the form of the building should be so complete in its beauty that additions would spoil that form," a stipulation invoked more than twenty years later to defeat plans for expanding the gallery.[5]

While the roofs conveyed the impression of vaults, those over the galleries were in fact concrete beams with half arches that sprang from them to form the vault shape. They were devised in consultation with Kahn's long-serving engineer, August Komendant, who separated them at their point of meeting with a two-foot-wide slot that channeled sunlight to an aluminum reflector pierced by tiny holes and suspended just beneath the opening. The reflector — developed with the help of Marshall Meyers, who became Kahn's project architect, as well as Richard Kelly, who had worked with Kahn on the lighting for the Yale gallery and at Exeter — was a triumph of ingenuity. It received direct sunlight, but then simultaneously filtered and diverted it onto the concrete of the curved ceilings, which had been refined by Kahn's colleague Fred Langford to a smoothness exceeding even that at Salk. The effect was an almost ethereal atmosphere that protected the works of art from direct sun, but afforded them the most advantageous illumination.

Just as the Richards laboratories had been praised for what many saw as their historicizing forms, the Kimbell's "vaults" were interpreted by supporters as yet another example of Kahn delving into the architectural past — in this case that of ancient Rome. But, as at Richards, there was considerable sleight of hand involved. A critic for the *Kansas City Star* declared that there was "something wrong with a vault that isn't a vault. Kahn has taken an ancient form — or a form secondhand from Le Corbusier — and has debased it through the marvels of contemporary structural engineering."[6] The attack recalled Reyner Banham's critique of the hollow towers in Philadelphia. But like those criticisms, this one was offset by the visual and

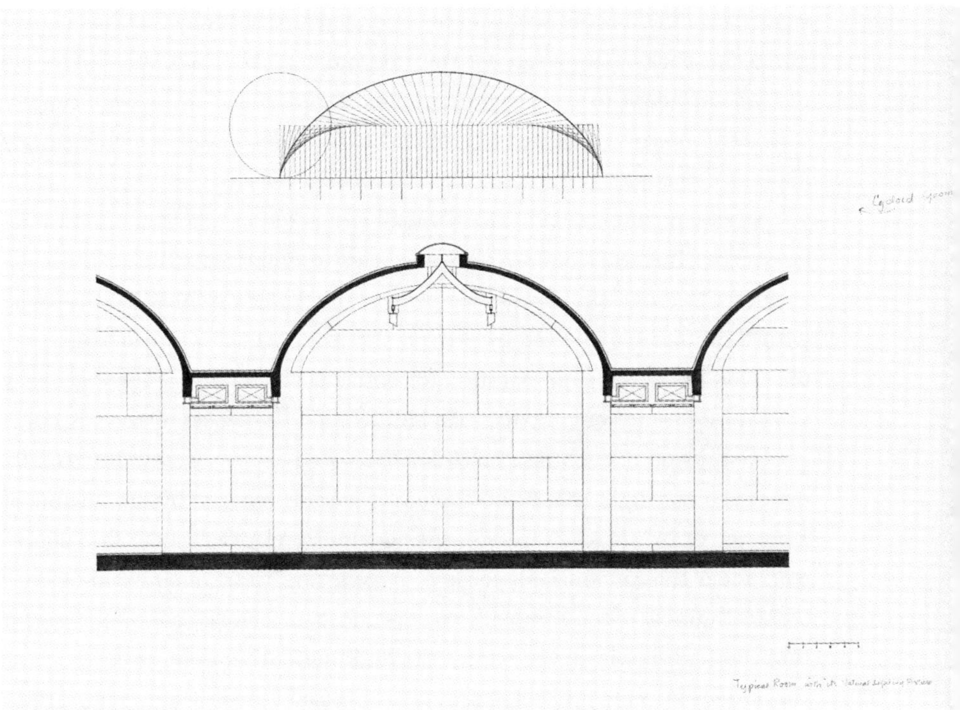

FIGURE 28. Section of Kimbell's "vault" that was actually a structural beam. (Louis I. Kahn Collection, University of Pennsylvania and Pennsylvania Historical and Museum Collection)

emotional power of the evocative forms. As Patricia Cummings Loud, the former curator of architecture at the Kimbell, explained: "Kahn's attitude toward this aspect of architecture was humanistic: he embraced the structuralist belief in honesty of structural expression, but realized that at times human interpretation of expression rules structure."[7]

In what was becoming a familiar palette of materials, Kahn designed doors of white oak, floors of travertine, and occasional panels of brushed stainless steel (see color plate 10) for the Kimbell's interior. The details of the materials were even more carefully wrought than those at Salk, and in working on them Kahn seems to have refined a philosophy that had its origins as far back as the design for the Yale Gallery. "The joint," he said in one of his semi-poetic pronouncements about the Kimbell, "is the beginning of ornament. And that must be distinguished from decoration which is simply applied. Ornament is the adoration of the joint."[8]

A critical component of the Kimbell composition was its setting in the landscape. This was done with great subtlety by George Patton, a landscape architect in Philadelphia who had been at the American Academy in Rome with Kahn in 1951, assisted by Harriet Pattison. "At the Kimbell Museum," observed Loud, "all is preparation for entering the building. The journey is made physical not only in distance but through the senses. One walks over grass, steps on crunching gravel, hears as well as sees water. The usually brilliant Texas light that Kahn thought silvery is relieved by the shadow of a portico or by the small trees in the court. Gravel gives way to firm aggregate under the entrance portico and, once inside, to travertine and wood."[9] Ironically, most of the Kimbell's visitors chose to arrive by car, which meant that they entered from the rear of the building, rather than walking across the elegant forecourt to which Kahn, Patton, and Pattison had devoted their artistry.

The museum opened in the first week of October 1972. *Newsweek* magazine, echoing the view of many critics, pronounced Kimbell "arguably the most beautiful museum in America."

As the Kimbell was nearing completion, Kahn received his final opportunity to create an environment for art, his original calling. Unlike the Kimbell, the Yale Center for British Art was intended to house a collection with a distinct focus. The client for what was originally called the Paul Mellon Center for British Art and British Studies was officially Yale University, but the donor was a powerful, if restrained, presence. Paul Mellon, an American aristocrat like George Howe, could not have been more dissimilar from Kahn, or from Jonas Salk. His father, Andrew Mellon, was an immensely

COLOR PLATE 1. The castle on the island of Saarema in Estonia, where Kahn was born. (Saarema Museum, photograph by Kristina Mägi)

COLOR PLATE 2. Yale's Branford Courtyard and Harkness Tower, by James Gamble Rogers (1917). (Manuscripts and Archives, Yale University Library)

COLOR PLATE 3. Interior of Kahn's Yale Art Gallery addition, showing the concrete "space frame" ceiling. (Louis I. Kahn Collection, University of Pennsylvania and Pennsylvania Historical and Museum Commission)

COLOR PLATE 4. The Esherick House, one of Kahn's residential designs that served as explorations for his bigger commissions. (Willliam J. Whitaker, Photographer)

COLOR PLATE 5. Kahn with Jonas Salk, a "soul mate" who remained his favorite client, at the Salk Institute. (Phillip Harrington / Alamy Stock Photo)

COLOR PLATE 6. The Salk plaza, showing the study towers for institute fellows. (Carol M. Highsmith Archive, Library of Congress, Prints and Photographs Division)

COLOR PLATE 7. Exterior of the deceptively simple Phillips Exeter Academy library. (Phillips Exeter Academy)

COLOR PLATE 8. The library atrium, a virtuoso display of Kahn's concealed theatricality. (Photograph by John W. Hession)

COLOR PLATE 9. The Kimbell Art Museum evoked Roman themes. (Carol M. Highsmith Archive, Library of Congress, Prints and Photographs Division)

COLOR PLATE 10. Kimbell gallery, showing the ceiling-mounted light diffuser. (Photograph by Robert LaPrelle, © 2013 Kimbell Art Museum, Fort Worth)

COLOR PLATE 11. The Yale Center for British Art main gallery with its concrete stair tower. (Michael Marsland/Yale University)

COLOR PLATE 12. Kahn's First Unitarian Church of Rochester, New York. (John Dorio Nicolais Collection, The Architectural Archives, University of Pennsylvania)

COLOR PLATE 13. A typical interior court of the Indian Institute of Management. (Indian Institute of Management Ahmedabad)

COLOR PLATE 14. The main Dhaka building from its artificial pond. (© Roberto Schezen/Esto)

COLOR PLATE 15. Interior of the Dhaka parliament building. (Photograph by Grischa Rüschendorf/Rupho)

COLOR PLATE 16. The main stair of the Roosevelt Island memorial. (© 2012 Paul Warchol)

FIGURE 29. Paul Mellon, Kahn's elegantly unlikely patron for the Yale Center for British Art. (Office of Public Affairs, Yale University, Photographs of Individuals [RU 686], Manuscripts and Archives, Yale University Library; Michael Marsland, photographer)

wealthy Pittsburgh banker who had funded the National Gallery of Art in Washington, D.C., and although he differed with Franklin Roosevelt politically and financially, became secretary of the treasury. The senior Mellon sent his son to Yale, where he rowed on the lightweight crew and wrote poetry for the college literary magazine. To his father's dismay, Paul was not interested in banking, and after graduation from Yale went on to Cambridge University, where he fell in love with virtually everything English. Beginning with the purchase of a small painting by the eighteenth-century painter George Stubbs, the younger Mellon assembled what became the largest collection of British art outside the United Kingdom. In 1966, he announced that he would be leaving his collection to Yale, along with enough money to build and endow a museum to house it. An unusual but important aspect of Mellon's bequest was that it should include a study center as well as galleries for the display of his paintings and sculptures.

Mellon had commissioned I. M. Pei to design the addition to the National Gallery of Art, and might have urged Yale to select Pei if he had been available, but since he was not, Mellon left the choice for the New Haven project in the university's hands. When the search began, Vincent Scully, who had all but discovered Louis Kahn as a major talent, had shifted his enthusiasm to Robert Venturi, the author of *Complexity and Contradiction in Architecture* and a seminal figure in the rise of postmodernism, and urged Yale to give him the commission. Despite Scully's singular influence,

Yale broadened its search, turning the process over to Jules David Prown, a Harvard-trained art historian and tenured member of the faculty. In a report to Yale's president, Kingman Brewster, Prown described the requirements of the building in terms remarkably like those others had applied to the Kimbell: "In a word the building must be humanistic, especially in order that the understanding and response of the museum visitor to British art be enhanced by his own life experience while viewing it."[10]

Like Rodney Armstrong at Exeter, Prown quickly identified Kahn as the best candidate, but not without reservations. He had contacted Richard Brown at the Kimbell to ask what it was like to work with Kahn, and Brown replied, "It was a lot of trouble, but it was worth it."[11] Prown was willing to take the risk, and became both Kahn's advocate and his protector, defending the architect as costs mounted and delays multiplied, while pressing him to develop a design that would match the ambitions of both donor and institution. Reflecting on the experience in 2009, Prown concluded that "the building embodies a system of values that quietly but insistently promotes Louis Kahn's moral philosophy. For him, architecture is about ethics; every decision in its making, large or small, represents a choice between right and wrong, true and false. His building insistently, even didactically, asserts truth as a primary virtue."[12]

The location for what became known as the Yale Center for British Art (YCBA) presented a variety of problems, not all of them physical. Since its move to New Haven in the eighteenth century, Yale had developed a tense relationship with its host city. As the university expanded, New Haven became increasingly sensitive to Yale's acquisition of city property, which would be lost to the tax rolls. The tension had already contributed to New Haven's rejection of a proposed residential college. The site for the Mellon building lay across Chapel Street, which had been seen for years as a symbolic moat separating Yale College from the rest of the city. It also lay across from Kahn's first building, his addition to the university's art gallery, afford-

FIGURE 30. The street façade of the YCBA in 2019, showing the metal cladding with its deliberate discoloration. (Michael Marsland/Yale University)

ing him an opportunity to demonstrate his artistic progress at the risk of disappointing expectations.

In addition to space for the display of works of art, the program for the YCBA called for a study area where students and scholars could delve deeper into the collection, which included prints, drawings, and books. The dual mission of the building provided Kahn a seemingly welcome challenge to combine elements of Kimbell, a pure museum, with elements of both the Exeter library and the unbuilt meeting house at Salk, where scholarship and creative thinking had been the goal of the design. Prown described Exeter and Kimbell as "the parents" of the British Art Center.[13]

The architect quickly embraced the complex commission. "Kahn's greatest gift," Prown recalled years later, "was his remarkable ability to grasp, almost to feel, the most elemental aspects of a problem. His sometimes startling and memorably expressed understanding of the nature of man and materials, their attributes, requirements, and limitations, seemed to derive from an intuitive sense of the primal."[14] An example of this ability is the way the architect managed here to evoke the elegantly residential atmosphere of English country houses, where many of Mellon's paintings had once hung, without imitating any of their traditional features. Noting the frequency with which Kahn mentioned fireplaces in his comments about the building, one scholar has speculated that the enormous concrete silo that encloses the building's main staircase and dominates the second-floor gallery is an intuitive reference to the hearths that provide the focus for so many great houses in England (see color plate 11).[15]

After Yale rejected several designs as too large or too expensive, Kahn settled on a four-story building focused on two interior courts that recalled the atrium space at Exeter. The entrance, rather than centered on the long façade as it had been in earlier schemes, was tucked under a corner, in part because Yale's president wanted the building to be seen as welcoming toward both Yale and New Haven. Another reason for this orientation may have been that, as at Exeter, a conventional entrance would have compromised the geometric integrity of the form. The stately organization—ten bays by six enclosing clearly delineated galleries—recalled Kahn's Beaux-Arts training under Paul Cret at Penn. But the delicate juxtaposition of concrete with white oak and linen wall coverings and carpets of natural wool created a surprisingly intimate sense of domesticity.

Although the inclusion of shops on the ground floor of the YCBA had been proposed by Yale as a strategy to pacify New Haven authorities concerned about losing tax revenues, Kahn did not object; this is not surprising, as he may have found that integrating scholarly and commercial activity added to the appeal of the building as an integral part of its urban surroundings. Perhaps the most surprising choice Kahn made for the building was to clad it in panels of dark stainless steel. Metal was in almost every way an unconventional choice, and risked giving the YCBA an industrial aspect. But Kahn clearly anticipated the effect of weathering on the material, which changed color over time and gradually developed a patina that became yet another subtle form of ornament. Kahn referred to the material as having the appearance of pewter or lead; one of his most quoted observations defending the steel cladding was that "on a gray day, it will look like a moth; on a sunny day like a butterfly."[16]

Controlling the light for the YCBA presented an entirely different set of problems from those Kahn had faced in Fort Worth. There, the challenge had been to modulate an excess of sunlight; in the changeable weather of New England, the problem was how to capture enough natural light to illuminate the galleries without relying too heavily on electricity. Working again with Richard Kelly, Kahn developed a coordinated system of light monitors and louvers to admit maximum daylight, and a network of incandescent electric fixtures that would increase or decrease the amount of artificial light according to changing conditions. This hybrid approach meant that the amount of daylight entering the building would remain relatively constant through the day, regardless of the season.

Here too, as he had at the original Yale gallery, Exeter, and Kimbell, Kahn found ways to combine his sense of visual drama with utilitarian necessities. Perhaps the most striking example at the YCBA was his threading of air-handling ducts through the hollow interior of what appeared to be structural beams on the fourth floor. Kahn's ally in the engineering of the YCBA was not August Komendant but Abba Tor, an irreverent Israeli who had joined forces with Henry Pfisterer, the engineer who had worked with Kahn on the Yale Art Gallery. Tor became adept at restraining Kahn's habit of trying to make design changes well past deadlines, and was not above invoking some mocking humor when the architect indulged his mystical musings. A favorite target of Tor's barbs was Kahn's much-repeated aphorism about the importance of using materials in appropriate ways. The architect was often quoted as saying: "I say to brick, 'What do you like, brick?' Brick says: 'I like an arch.'" Tor would have none of it, and kidded Kahn by saying, "Lou, what did the wall say the last time you talked to it?"[17]

On March 17, 1974, Kahn was returning from a trip to India when he suffered a heart attack and died in New York City's Pennsylvania Station. His death shocked the architectural community and everyone who knew or worked with him, not least the team involved with the YCBA. Although the fundamental design was complete and construction well under way, much was left undone, including the final design of the light monitors, and such smaller details as the stair railings. Yale appointed Pellecchia and Meyers, a firm whose partner Marshall Meyers had been a close associate and the project architect on the Kimbell. Sorting out the unfinished business took another two years, and the Yale Center for British Art opened on April 15, 1977. Hovering over every decision was the question: "What would Lou do?" One of the more amusing examples was the dispute over how to proceed when a sliver of concrete fell off the exposed column at the YBCA's entrance. Yale was not about to countenance such a flaw at the entrance to a building of such importance, and one funded by such a patron. But some Kahn loyalists argued that the blemish should be left, claiming that the architect would have wanted an honest expression of architecture's inevitable imperfections. Yale prevailed, and the concrete was patched.

One of Kahn's accomplishments about which there was no dispute was his ability to combine his passions and document his progress as an architect with an almost uncanny symmetry. In 1952, with his addition to the Yale University Art Gallery at the corner of Chapel and York Streets in New

Haven, Connecticut, Louis Kahn had emerged as an architect of promise. Slightly over twenty years later, and just across the street, he displayed almost all that he had learned in the intervening time. What remained would be summed up in a series of buildings that went beyond their functional programs to an even higher realm.

EIGHT | AN ARCHITECTURE OF ASPIRATION

Although Louis Kahn was born into a Jewish family, religion never played a major role in his personal life. He did not normally attend religious services, and only occasionally observed Jewish holidays with his family. Kahn's wife was Jewish, but the mothers of his two out-of-wedlock children were both Protestant. Apart from Jonas Salk, his major patrons — George Howe in Philadelphia, G. Holmes Perkins at Penn, Rodney Armstrong at Exeter, Richard Brown in Fort Worth, Paul Mellon at Yale — were pillars of the WASP establishment, yet Kahn never showed any enthusiasm for conventional Christianity. Nevertheless, there was something unmistakably suprarational about much of Kahn's best work. It did not manifest itself in literal symbolism, but was communicated through architectural devices Kahn employed to create forms and spaces that inspired both awe and serenity. These are characteristics of the greatest houses of worship, but in Kahn's hands they were not limited to religious institutions. Indeed, three of Kahn's completed projects that best illustrate what he called a sense of aspiration in his architecture were dedicated to business, politics, and human rights.

The first indication that Kahn was an architect of spaces that transcended their program can be traced to the bathhouse for the Jewish Community Center in Trenton, New Jersey. Although the building was probably the smallest he ever designed, its clear organization and basic forms displayed a new confidence in his aesthetic vocabulary that Kahn himself recognized, if only in retrospect. Reflecting on his career in 1970, he observed,

"If the world discovered me after I designed the Richards towers building, I discovered myself after designing that little concrete-block bathhouse in Trenton."[1] The building, commissioned in 1955, was finished in 1959, the same year that Kahn was invited to design a building for the First Unitarian Church of Rochester, New York. Unitarianism, which accepts members of all faiths, seems to have had a special appeal for Kahn, since it came close to his undefined sense of religion as rooted in feeling rather than doctrine.[2] According to a member of the congregation in Rochester who helped select the architect, "The idea that we welcomed everyone intrigued him."[3] Speaking about his concept for the church, Kahn said, somewhat cryptically, "Having heard the minister give a sense of the Unitarian aspirations, it occurred to me that the sanctuary is merely the center of the questions."[4] Kahn might have used the word "faith," or "religion," or even "doctrine"—his choice of "aspirations" suggested that he had made a connection with his clients that went beyond denominational limitations.

When completed in 1969, the building presented a slightly forbidding exterior of boxy brick shapes pierced by vertical slots for windows (see color plate 12), evoking images of the medieval fortresses Kahn had sketched on his European trips. The interior, however, strikes a much softer note. Indirect light admitted through clerestory windows in four corner towers animates a large space for the congregation within a ring of offices and rooms for the church school. Consistent with Unitarian doctrine, there is no altar. The light in the sanctuary is not as sensitively modulated as in the Kimbell or the YCBA, but here the intent is clearly to create a contemplative experience, one dedicated to the spirit, rather than to illuminate works of art.

Kahn had a chance to honor his own religious heritage in 1961 with a commission for the Mikveh Israel congregation in Philadelphia. The project had a special significance because it meant restoring a Jewish religious presence in the historic part of the city, not far from the site of Philadelphia's first synagogue, whose congregation was established in 1740. The design went through six iterations, none of which was executed. Kahn was dismissed by the congregation in 1972, officially because the project had run out of money, and though he lost many commissions, this was reportedly one of the most painful.[5]

Ironically, Kahn's most intense exposure to religious tradition did not involve Judaism or Christianity, but the spiritual beliefs and traditions of South Asia. In 1961, just as Kahn was beginning his ill-fated work on Mikveh Israel, he was contacted by Balkrishna Doshi, an Indian architect he had met when Doshi was lecturing at the University of Pennsylvania. Doshi had worked with Le Corbusier on the design of Chandigarh, the majestic new capital of the Indian state of Punjab, begun in 1952. Largely due to that experience, he had been asked by the Indian government to collaborate with a number of prominent business leaders to develop an institution in the northern city of Ahmedabad to train Indians in management skills, modeled on the Harvard Business School, which supported the Indian initiative. While patterned on the Harvard curriculum, the mission of the Indian Institute of Management was not solely to produce successful businessmen but also to train leaders of a nation that was steadily growing in economic and political influence. Doshi was asked to design IIM himself, but after developing the program, he urged the sponsors to find an architect of greater international reputation in order, as he put it, to "make Ahmedabad a world heritage site of contemporary architecture."[6] He proposed Kahn, who was offered the commission with the understanding that Doshi would be the intermediary between client and architect, much as Rodney Armstrong had been at Exeter and Jules Prown had been at the Yale Center for British Art.

Kahn had never been to India, and he knew little about its social, religious, or architectural traditions, so Doshi took it upon himself to give the American a tutorial in Indian culture. This involved visiting the major monuments of the subcontinent's architectural history, ranging from ancient temples to contemporary residences, where Kahn was exposed to

FIGURE 31. The main entrance to the Indian Institute of Management in Ahmedabad. (Indian Institute of Management Ahmedabad)

traditional forms and the ingenious ways in which Indian architects had dealt with the intense sunlight of the region. But the tutorial gradually took on another dimension. Doshi had a strong personal interest in spirituality, and as his relationship with Kahn grew deeper, he came to appreciate his colleague's enduring commitment to the betterment of the human condition. "He understood the sacredness of life," Doshi recalled. "I talked to him about destiny, about karma, about spiritual value."[7] The experience seems to have resonated with Kahn. Anant Raje, an Indian architect who became an important member of the IIM team and worked in Kahn's Philadelphia office, noted that when Kahn was leaving America on a trip to Ahmedabad, he would say to his staff, "Now I'm going to India, where I am understood."[8] The effect was mutual. Reflecting on his interactions with Kahn in 2004,

Doshi observed, "We thought that in an earlier incarnation he had been an Indian saint, a yogi. He was talking the way we talked."[9]

As built, the IIM campus comprised classrooms, dormitories, and faculty quarters, rendered primarily in brick, but with delicate concrete flourishes that identified doors, windows, and floor levels. The complex, which is entered by climbing a grand staircase, is focused on an open courtyard. Empty of students, the campus has an atmosphere of timeless mass, echoing the ruins that attracted Kahn on his visit to Rome in 1950–51. That impression is amplified by the architect's use of enormous circular cutouts in the brick walls that recall the drama of the Exeter atrium, but here elevate the composition to an almost intimidating level of visual abstraction (see color plate 13). When the IIM is in session, however, it teems with activity, suggesting the hurly-burly of daily life in the clogged markets of Ahmedabad, or perhaps the bustling streets of Philadelphia's Northern Liberties when Kahn was a child.

The IIM is at once a striking combination of stately architectural order bearing an almost Beaux-Arts gravity and an environment for random human interaction. Tucked among the looming brick boxes housing the classrooms are small bridges, walkways, and courtyards that encourage unexpected encounters. The complex seems to be sending a message of high professional ambition, while at the same time recognizing the chaotic nature of student life. Although the IIM was designed as a self-contained campus with a specific mission, it was executed in a way that enhances exploration. Looking back on his experience with Le Corbusier in designing Chandigarh, Doshi told an interviewer in 1986, "I think 20 years hence Chandigarh may not even be considered an Indian city, because it gives us Le Corbusier's sense of the future but not of Indian life . . . you have streets, open spaces, houses — but you have no life!"[10] Here, Kahn had managed to absorb the lessons of Indian life and infuse them into his architecture.

While working on the IIM, Kahn was also engaged in an even more ambitious project to the east. In 1947, after the British partition of India, Pakistan emerged as an independent nation, but one that was geographically divided into eastern and western sectors. The country's military ruler, whose seat of government was to the west in Islamabad, decided that he could maintain better control of his country by adding a second capital in East Pakistan, in the city of Dhaka, a center of Bengali culture. The design of the capital buildings was offered to Muzharul Islam, a Bengali architect who had trained at the University of Oregon, the Architectural Association in London, and Yale, where his studio was located in Kahn's addition to the art gallery. (He was the only formally trained architect in Pakistan, where most buildings were designed by engineers.) Like Doshi, Islam advised his client to select an architect of greater international reputation to give the project sufficient stature. When Le Corbusier and the Finnish master Alvar Aalto proved unavailable, Kahn was offered the job.

Echoing Doshi, Islam felt that Kahn needed an immersion in local architectural traditions in order to produce an appropriate design. Accordingly, he provided Kahn with a small library of books on Bengali history and took him on extended tours of ancient Mughal monuments, pointing out the special characteristics of the surrounding landscape and the clustering of buildings on earthen mounds to avoid the annual floods. If the IIM was intended to train emerging business and political leaders, the campus of what came to be known as Sher-e-Bangla Nagar ("City of the Tiger") was to serve the governmental needs of an entire population. Kahn was so enthusiastic about the possibilities of the commission that he persuaded the Pakistani government to expand the site from two hundred to nearly one thousand acres. Not since his speculative city projects for Philadelphia in the 1950s had he been given an opportunity to indulge his interest in urban planning, but in this case the mission was not merely to sort out the traffic patterns of an American city but to create an entirely new cultural center. In addition to an assembly building, which would house the main parliamentary func-

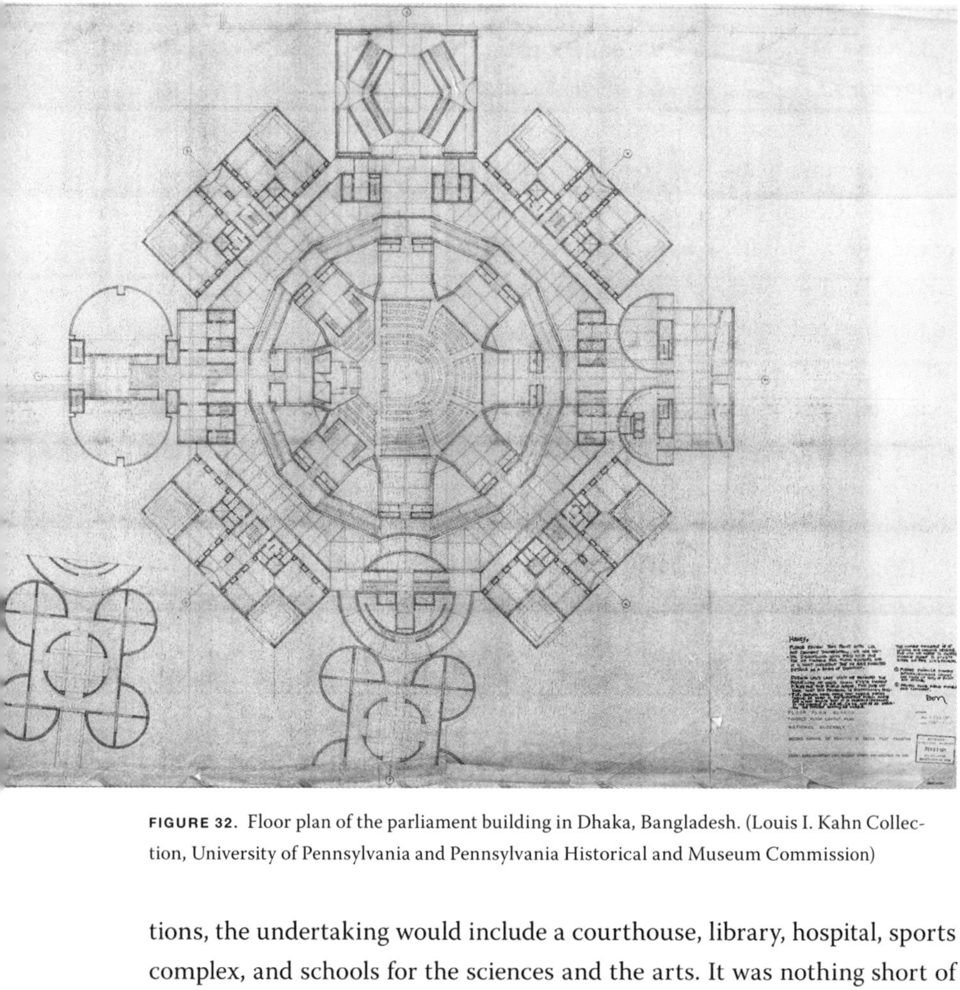

FIGURE 32. Floor plan of the parliament building in Dhaka, Bangladesh. (Louis I. Kahn Collection, University of Pennsylvania and Pennsylvania Historical and Museum Commission)

tions, the undertaking would include a courthouse, library, hospital, sports complex, and schools for the sciences and the arts. It was nothing short of an ideal community at an unprecedented scale, more than fulfilling ambitions that had been frustrated at Salk.

In the end, the cultural amenities were gradually stripped from the Dhaka program, leaving only the government center and its support buildings. But even at a reduced scale, Kahn's work represents a staggering architectural achievement. And more than at Ahmedabad, Kahn seems to have been able to absorb the architectural precedents of the region—especially those involving the treatment of natural light—and reinterpret them in a modern idiom. He was encouraged in his efforts by Muzharul Islam, who was not merely an architect but also a dedicated socialist with high hopes for his country's political future.

The centerpiece of the Dhaka complex as built is a diamond-shaped ten-story concrete structure with an assembly hall at the core (see color plate 14). Surrounding this, a hallway opens onto semi-detached units for offices and services. The symmetrical layout and layered separation of functions recall many of Kahn's earlier designs, most notably the Exeter library, the First Unitarian Church, and unexecuted projects for a congress hall in Venice and a synagogue in Jerusalem. Kahn must have been pleased that the program for the Dhaka building included a "meditation place." Although East Pakistan was largely Muslim, it was home to many other religions, and Kahn accommodated this diverse spirituality by describing the space as a "prayer hall," as well as a mosque. (It was, however, gently moved off the axis of the main building to align more closely with Mecca.)

On the north side of the complex, Kahn included a large ceremonial plaza. The exterior walls were set forward from the core and pierced by enormous openings in the form of rectangles, circles, and triangles, expanding on the design devices he had tested at Exeter and was employing in Ahmedabad (see color plate 15). These gave the building a vaguely anthropomorphic appearance, as if it were some sort of giant mask. But they also admitted light to the circular hallway, which functioned as an interior street, or ambulatory, while protecting the delegates from direct sun. A dizzying maze of staircases and ramps opened onto the ambulatory, expanding on Exeter's scheme, where users could see other occupants as they went about their work. The overwhelming mass of the structure was visually mitigated, both inside and out, by thin strips of marble applied both horizontally and vertically. (These were originally used to conceal the joints between the sections of concrete poured in a single day, but Kahn threaded them throughout the building for ornamental effect.) The main structure is surrounded by an artificial lake, an homage to the local tradition of building above the flood plain. Arrayed around the lake were intimate clusters of townhouses and other small buildings designed for delegates and visitors.

The residences, clad in brick, create a clear visual hierarchy with the more authoritative concrete assembly building, and suggest a community that has grown up around its central gathering place. Even more than the IIM, the Dhaka complex embodies Kahn's aspiration for an ideal social environment, the origins of which can be traced back to the Mackley Houses, Carver Court, Jersey Homesteads, and the other low-cost housing projects he had designed in the 1930s and 1940s. But in Dhaka the organization creates a sense of elemental civilization, of people gathering around, and linked to, an institution dedicated to their welfare. Kahn repeatedly cited the Baths of Caracalla in Rome as a model for the assembly building, but his inspiration was clearly more abstract and far-reaching. In a letter he wrote as part of his unsuccessful bid to design the John F. Kennedy Library in Dorchester, Massachusetts, he concluded that "the complicated requirements took form out of the realization that assembly is a religious act . . . that the acts of assembly are the making of the institution of man."[11]

However firm the motivation behind Kahn's work in Dhaka, it was threatened in 1971, when a nine-month war of independence broke out between West and East Pakistan (in which the United States supported West Pakistan). The conflict forced Kahn to close the Dhaka field office for nearly a year, but he did not stop working on the design, and when work resumed under the newly independent state of Bangladesh, much of the original scheme was abandoned. Although he wouldn't have welcomed the bloody upheaval that led to Pakistan's division, he could take some satisfaction in knowing that his buildings would now serve not as a secondary capital but as the governmental center of an entirely new nation. Incomplete as it was, Sher-e-Bangla Nagar came close to fulfilling Kahn's persistent dream of creating a community in the full sense of the word. In contrast to the work of Le Corbusier at Chandigarh, which as Balkrishna Doshi had pointed out was considered somewhat alien to the Indian environment, Kahn's buildings at Dhaka were immediately embraced as appropriate to the culture they served. They also exerted an influence on the people's attitude toward government. As a Bangladeshi architect observed after the assembly building had been in use for decades, "When parliament was out of session, the building stood like our conscience, watching us, waiting for us to do the right thing."[12] There was no better proof of the building's impact on its populace than the Bangladesh government's decision to include an image of the assembly on its currency as a symbol of the emergent nation's stature.

Louis Kahn died before he could see his project in Dhaka to completion; it was not declared finished until 1983, even though much of the original scheme was unrealized and would never be complete. In a bizarre development, another of Kahn's projects, which had been abandoned, then revived, would provide a coda to the ideals he had been pursuing from his days as a young architect to the lofty aspirations of the Bangladesh capital.

Though what eventually emerged as the Franklin D. Roosevelt Four Freedoms Park on Roosevelt Island in New York City was much closer to home than Dhaka, it nonetheless was in some ways located in more alien territory. Kahn had never liked New York, feeling that it was too concerned with power and money; Philadelphia's small scale and welcoming Quakerism seemed to suit him better. But he did have a deeply personal, if distant, connection to the project. When Kahn was thirty-two, Franklin Delano Roosevelt, the former governor of New York State, was elected president of the United States. Virtually everything that FDR's progressive agenda addressed was something about which Kahn cared passionately, especially low-cost housing. More important, surely, was Roosevelt's dedication to the cause of freedom and the protection of human rights, which had always been part of Kahn's consciousness even if he did not articulate them in political terms. In several ways, the poverty-stricken immigrant from an oppressed religious minority owed his eventual success to the policies FDR had championed. According to Kahn's daughter Sue Ann, "The betterment of mankind was a paramount theme among my parents' circle of friends and colleagues . . . Many of the projects [my father] worked on or spearheaded were funded by Roosevelt's Public Works Administration, Resettlement Administration, and other arms of the New Deal."[13] So when Kahn was contacted in 1973 to design a memorial to Roosevelt in New York City, he did not hesitate. (He may also have been subtly influenced by the fact that the late president had been a polio victim, and that Kahn's most receptive client, Jonas Salk, had helped to conquer the disease.)

The contact came through William Walton who, fresh from advising the Kennedy family on Dorchester's JFK Library (designed by I. M. Pei), had become head of the Fine Arts Commission in Washington, D.C. Edward Logue, then head of New York State's Urban Development Corporation, asked Walton for names of candidates, and Walton, who had come to know Kahn during the competition for the Kennedy library commission, recommended him, observing that Kahn "remembers FDR with insight and reverence."[14]

The inspiration for the project was the speech Roosevelt delivered to the U.S. Congress on January 6, 1941, looking forward to "a world founded upon four essential human freedoms." These were "freedom of speech and expression," "freedom of every person to worship God in his own way," "freedom from want," and "freedom from fear."

The design, which Kahn created working with Harriet Pattison, was a model of simplicity, order, and delicacy. As built, it forms an elongated triangle at the southern end of Welfare Island—renamed Roosevelt Island—

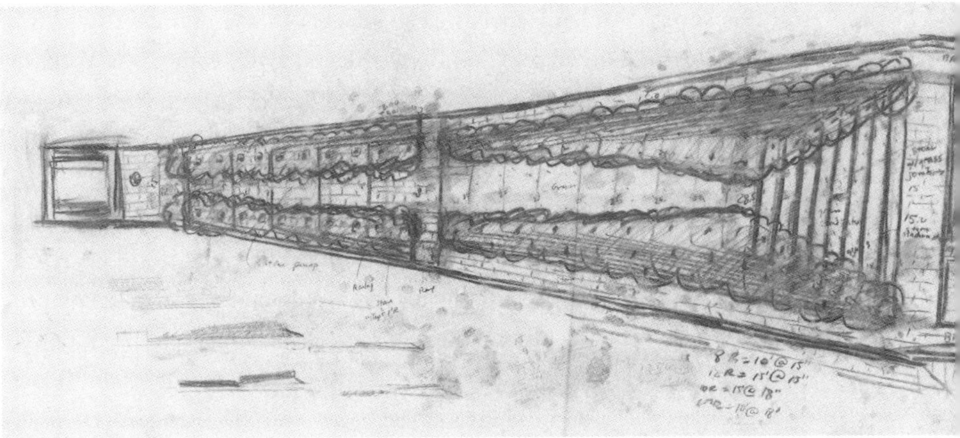

FIGURE 33. Preliminary sketch for the Franklin D. Roosevelt Four Freedoms Park on New York City's Roosevelt Island. (Harriet Pattison Collection, The Architectural Archives, University of Pennsylvania)

a narrow sliver of land running north to south in New York's East River roughly opposite the headquarters of the United Nations. Kahn exploited the shape of the site by creating a broad, gently rising staircase at the northern end and filling the center with two double rows of trees flanking a lawn that descends to an open-ended "room" at the southern tip of the island (see color plate 16). The northern wall of the room opens around a rectangular block with an oversized bronze bust of Roosevelt by the sculptor Jo Davidson. The words of Roosevelt's speech are inscribed on the south facade. The primary elements of the memorial are massive blocks of granite, which form the walls bordering the lawn and enclose the room. Not long after Kahn died, the city was beset by a financial crisis, and plans for the memorial were shelved.

The person most responsible for realizing the Roosevelt memorial was William vanden Heuvel, a native of Rochester, New York. Like Kahn, he was a son of European immigrants, and as a boy had developed a fascination with Roosevelt. Vanden Heuvel was so affected by the president's death in 1945 that he hitchhiked four hundred miles to Hyde Park, New York, for FDR's funeral. When the Secret Service tried to block him from attending, the fourteen-year-old noticed the Roosevelt's widow, Eleanor, in the crowd and told her his story. She allowed him to stay. The gesture made vanden Heuvel a lifelong advocate for FDR, and when the Kahn project was revived, he spearheaded the raising of nearly $60 million to build it.

Supervised by Gina Pollara, the project architect, the construction process weathered the inevitable questions involved in completing a design after its architect's death, especially when the architect was given to last-minute changes. As was the case at the Yale Center for British Art, all involved were anxious about "What Lou would do."[15]

While the work proceeded, the construction crew noticed that a small harbor seal had been surfacing each day on the tiny outcropping of rock just south of the island. And though the seal's appearance may have affirmed the improved quality of the water in the famously polluted East River, the workers felt there was more involved and decided to adopt the animal as the project's mascot. Soon enough, they held a vote whether to name the seal "Frank" for the president or "Louie," for the architect. Louie won.

The Kahn design that is most often compared to the Franklin D. Roosevelt Four Freedoms Park is the Salk Institute, which is known less for its laboratories than for its open courtyard, a space that provokes strong emotional reactions through its simplicity and its relationship to nature. Although the programs of the two works differ, they have in common what vanden Heuvel calls "the universal expression of great ideas. Spirituality is the most important thing about it."[16] When the FDR memorial opened to the public, in the fall of 2012, the *New York Times* architecture critic declared, "It gives New York nothing less than a new spiritual heart."[17]

According to vanden Heuvel, many of the visitors to the Four Freedoms Park return repeatedly, something it shares more in common with

FIGURE 34. Looking south toward Jo Davidson's bust of Franklin Delano Roosevelt. (© 2012 Paul Warchol)

Maya Lin's Vietnam Veterans Memorial in Washington, D.C., than with other such destinations. Indeed, much of the appeal of the Vietnam memorial is its abstraction, which does not prescribe visitors' responses with recognizable heroic figures but allows them to invest their own feelings in the monument. Well before Lin completed her design, Kahn seems to have understood that contemplation is more important to a lasting tribute than veneration.

The proximity of the Roosevelt memorial to the United Nations, the institution that continues to strive for a peaceful and equitable world—and was championed most vigorously by Eleanor Roosevelt—provides a remarkable symmetry to the Kahn saga. In many ways the Roosevelt project brought the architect's life full circle. He had come to the United States as a poor refugee whose parents were seeking a better life. He was rescued by a public education system guided by ideals of peace and inclusivity. Although his was a radically different social and economic background, Franklin Roosevelt had been dedicated to keeping Kahn's adopted country open to those fleeing oppression, and to improving the lot of the disadvantaged. The freedoms he espoused were nowhere established facts, even in the United States. They were conditions that demanded constant vigilance and continued support. They defined an ideal world, one very much like the one Louis I. Kahn had envisioned as a young, unemployed architect in Philadelphia, and came to refine as a servant of powerful institutions that sought to advance the greater good. The completion of the Roosevelt memorial seemed a fitting tribute to the durability of the ideals it enshrined, and to the idealism of the designer who gave it form.

Unique among his professional contemporaries, Kahn was able to combine his formal training in traditional Western architecture with an intuitive sense of historical memory. He added to this a message of moral commitment to the betterment of humankind. And he did it with consummate artistry.

ACKNOWLEDGMENTS

I would like to thank the following individuals, whose experience, expertise, recollections, and support helped to shape this account of Louis Kahn's life and work:

Rodney Armstrong
Edmund Bacon
Kenneth Borst
Donald Briselden
Duncan Buell
Earl Carlin
Peter Clement
Katharine Cortesi
Charles Dagit
Balkrishna Doshi
Jean France
Nicholas Gianopulos
Frances Halsband
Muzharul Islam
Nathaniel Kahn
Sue Ann Kahn
Daphne Kalomiris
Ishraq Khan
Nurur Rahman Khan
George Knight
Carol Krinsky
Reyhan Tansal Larimer
Nancy Lincoln
Patricia Cummings Loud
John MacAllister
Estelle Margolis
Michael Marsland
Shannon McGoldrick
Kate Mertes
Amy Meyers
Eugene Nalle
Leona Nalle
Herbert Newman
Allison Olsen
Harriet Pattison
G. Holmes Perkins
Gina Pollara
James Stewart Polshek

Jules David Prown
Alexander Purves
Anant Raje
David Rinehart
James G. Rogers III
Peter Salk
Charles Sawyer
Gail Scanlon
Judith Ann Schiff
Ludovica Schniewind
Vincent Scully
Priyanka Sheth
Robert A. M. Stern
Karen Tatarkas
Jacquelyn Thomas
Stanley Tigerman
Abba Tor
Alexandra Tyng
Anne Tyng
William vanden Heuvel
Shamsul Wares
William Whitaker
Henry Wilcots
Wizard

I would also like to thank my agent of many years, Sterling Lord, my patient editors Boyd Zenner and Mark Mones at the University of Virginia Press, and Anne Levine for her extraordinary help drawing together the illustrations.

In addition to these individuals, I am grateful to W. W. Norton, and especially Donald Lamm and Starling Lawrence, for their support of my earlier book on Louis Kahn, *Beyond Time and Style,* a biography published in 2007, and for Norton's generous consideration in the publication of this volume.

NOTES

Introduction

1. Christopher Hawthorne, "A Vast Louis Kahn Retrospective Lands at the San Diego Museum of Art," *Los Angeles Times,* Nov. 22, 2016.
2. Quoted in Kahn, *Louis Kahn, Essential Texts,* 253.
3. Katharine Cortesi, interview with the author, May 6, 2004.
4. Inga Saffron, "What the Brick Says," *New York Times,* April 23, 2017.
5. See Nicholas Fox Weber, *Le Corbusier, a Life* (New York: Alfred A. Knopf, 2008), 469.
6. Dietrich Neumann, interview with the author, February 1, 2017.

ONE | The Birth of a Vision

1. Roxanne Kuter Williamson, *American Architects and the Mechanics of Fame* (Austin: University of Texas Press, 1991), 4.
2. Tyng, *Beginnings,* 3.
3. Dagit, *Louis I. Kahn,* vii.
4. Dagit, *Louis I. Kahn,* xii.
5. Joseph A. Burton, "The Aesthetic Education of Louis I. Kahn, 1912–1924," *Perspecta 28, The Yale Architectural Journal* (Cambridge, Mass.: MIT Press, 1997), 205.
6. Kahn interview, *Pennsylvania Gazette,* December 1972, 19.
7. Elizabeth Greenwell Grossman, "Paul Cret," in *Macmillan Encyclopedia of Architects,* ed. Adolf K. Placzek (New York: Free Press, 1982), 1:476.
8. *University of Pennsylvania School of Fine Arts: Courses in Architecture Music and Fine Arts, Announcement 1922–23* (Philadelphia: The Press of the University of Pennsylvania), 18.
9. Elizabeth Greenwell Grossman, *Paul Philippe Cret: Rationalism and Imagery in American Architecture* (PhD diss., Brown University, 1980), 3.
10. Tyng, *Beginnings,* 9.

TWO | Shock to the System

1. Daniel Aaron, *Writers on the Left* (New York: Harcourt Brace & World, 1961), 63.
2. Marin Gottfried, *Arthur Miller: His Life and Work* (New York: Da Capo Press, 2003), 31.
3. Le Corbusier, *Towards a New Architecture* (New York: Praeger, 1965), 7.
4. Le Corbusier, *Towards a New Architecture,* 13.
5. Howard Zinn, *A People's History of the United States* (New York: Harper Collins, 2001), 393.
6. Walter Gropius, *The New Architecture and the Bauhaus* (New York: Museum of Modern Art, 1936), 59.
7. Chester Nagel, quoted in Wiseman, *I. M. Pei,* 43.
8. Henry-Russell Hitchcock and Philip Johnson, *The International Style* (New York: W. W. Norton, 1966), 20.
9. Hitchcock and Philip Johnson, *The International Style,* 30.
10. Ralph Adams Cram, *My Life in Architecture* (Boston: Little, Brown, 1936), 283.

THREE | Keeping the Faith

1. D. G. Coombs, Shell Eastern Petroleum Products, Inc., to Louis Kahn, December 4, 1930, Kahn Archives, University of Pennsylvania (hereafter Kahn Archives).
2. Office of Zantzinger, Borie & Medary to Louis Kahn, January 8, 1932, Kahn Archives.
3. Esther Kahn, personal journal, July 18, 1931; courtesy of Sue Ann Kahn.
4. Typescript of "Architecture and Modern Housing," January 6, 1933, Kahn Archives.
5. Stern, *George Howe,* 25.
6. See Tyng, *Beginnings,* 13.
7. "Outline of the Principles and Policies of the Society for the Advancement of Architecture," Kahn Archives.
8. "A.R.G. Submits Slum Clearance Scheme to Better Homes Exhibit," April 23, 1933, Kahn Archives.
9. Esther Kahn interview with Alessandra Latour, May 5, 1982.
10. Catherine Bauer, *Modern Housing* (Boston and New York: Houghton Mifflin, 1934), xvi.
11. ARG competition entry draft, Kahn Archives.

12. Bernard Newman to State Board of Examiners of Architects, Kahn Archives.
13. State Board of Examiners of Architects to Louis I. Kahn, August 10, 1934, Kahn Archives.
14. Bernard Newman to Louis Kahn, May 7, 1935, Kahn Archives.
15. Esther Kahn, personal journal; courtesy of Sue Anne Kahn.
16. See Kahn, *Louis I. Kahn: Writings, Lectures, Interviews,* 18.
17. Rykwert, *Louis Kahn,* 13.

FOUR | Right Time, Right Place

1. Stern and Stamp, *Pedagogy and Place,* xi.
2. Weiss, *The World of Art,* viii.
3. Quoted in Brownlee and DeLong, *Louis I. Kahn,* 54.
4. Quoted in Stern and Stamp, *Pedagogy and Place,* 99.
5. Gropius, *The New Architecture and the Bauhaus,* 17
6. Alofsin, *The Struggle for Modernism,* 154.
7. Quoted in Stern and Stamp, *Pedagogy and Place,* 121.
8. Herbert Newman, interview with the author, May 17, 2017.
9. Ludovica Schniewind, interview with the author, June 17, 2017.
10. Vincent Scully, interview with Alessandra Latour, editor, *Louis I. Kahn: L'uomo, il maestro* (Rome: Edizioni Kappa, 1986), 147.
11. Quoted in Stern and Stamp, *Pedagogy and Place,* 118.
12. Newman interview, May 17, 2017.

FIVE | Framing the Message

1. Charles Perry, undated, author's collection.
2. Peter Millard, interview with the author, October 14, 2004.
3. Gilbert, *Native Stone,* 60.
4. Alexander Purves, interview with the author, June 9, 2017.
5. Purves interview.
6. Schniewind, interview with the author.
7. Herbert Newman, interview with the author, May 18, 2017.
8. Earl Carlin, interview with the author, September 8, 2004.
9. James Polshek, interview with the author, June 11, 2017.
10. Carlin interview.
11. Estelle Margolis, interview with the author, May 11, 2004.

12. Frederick Gutheim, "Modern Architecture at Yale," *New York Herald Tribune,* November 28, 1953.
13. Vincent Scully, interview with the author, December 1, 2004.
14. J. Williamson, *Kahn at Penn,* 8.
15. Quoted in J. Williamson, *Kahn at Penn,* 9.
16. Quoted in J. Williamson, *Kahn at Penn,* 42.
17. J. Williamson, *Kahn at Penn,* 56.
18. Quoted in J. Williamson, *Kahn at Penn,* 24.
19. Dagit, *Louis I. Kahn,* 43.
20. J. Williamson, *Kahn at Penn,* 72.
21. Dagit, *Louis I. Kahn,* 63.
22. Komendant, *18 Years with Architect Louis I. Kahn,* 162.
23. Komendant, *18 Years with Architect Louis I. Kahn,* 162.
24. Scully interview.
25. Sue Ann Kahn, interview with the author, August 17, 2017.
26. J. Williamson, *Kahn at Penn,* 15
27. J. Williamson, *Kahn at Penn,* 3.
28. Dagit, *Louis I. Kahn,* 38.
29. Marcus and Whitaker, *The Houses of Louis Kahn,* 2.
30. Latour, editor, *Louis I. Kahn,* 31

SIX | Lessons in Learning

1. Quoted in Kahn, *Louis Kahn: Essential Texts,* 41.
2. Komendant, *18 Years with Architect Louis I. Kahn,* 8.
3. G. Holmes Perkins, interview with the author, May 13, 2004.
4. Komendant, *18 Years with Architect Louis I. Kahn,* 7.
5. Lobell, *Between Silence and Light,* 72.
6. Scully, *Louis I. Kahn,* 28.
7. Jordy, *American Buildings and Their Architects,* 362.
8. Reyner Banham, "The Buttery-Hatch Aesthetic," *Architectural Record,* March 1962, 205.
9. Komendant, *18 Years with Architect Louis I. Kahn,* 20.
10. John E. MacAllister, personal communication with the author, October 14, 2005.
11. Leslie, *Louis I. Kahn,* 117.

12. Jonas Salk, "Horizons into the Future," *Art and Antiques,* December 1990, 116.
13. Salk, "Horizons into the Future," 116.
14. Jonas Salk, "Architecture of Reality: Louis Kahn Memorial Lecture," American Institute of Architects, Philadelphia, Pennsylvania, April 5, 1984.
15. John MacAllister, interview with the author, June 23, 2005.
16. Thomas Albright, quoted in "Louis Kahn's Salk Institute" by Carolina Miranda, *Los Angeles Times,* November 22, 2016.
17. Elliot Gould Fish to Richard Day, July 23, 1965, Armstrong Papers, Phillips Exeter Academy Archives.
18. Quoted in Julia Heskell and Davis Dyer, *After the Harkness Gift* (Lebanon, N.H.: University Press of New England, 2008), 13.
19. Richard Saul Wurman used this as the title of his 1986 edited collection of Kahn's speeches, writings, interviews, and journal entries.
20. Rodney Armstrong, interview with the author, May 6, 2004.
21. Heskell and Dyer, *After the Harkness Gift,* 50.
22. Louis Kahn to Richard Day, August 18, 1966, Phillips Exeter Academy Archives.
23. Don Briselden, interview with the author, August 26, 2005.
24. Ada Louise Huxtable, "Exeter Library: Paean to Books," *New York Times,* October 23, 1972.

SEVEN | Art for Art's Sake

1. "America's Best Small Museum," Kimbell Art Museum, undated.
2. Quoted in Loud, *History of the Kimbell Art Museum,* 15.
3. Loud, *History of the Kimbell Art Museum,* 17.
4. Quoted in Johnson, *Light is the Theme,* 33.
5. Kimbell Art Museum, "Pre-architectural Program," June 1, 1966.
6. Quoted in Loud, *The Art Museums of Louis I. Kahn,* 158.
7. Loud, *The Art Museums of Louis I. Kahn,* 159.
8. Quoted in Johnson, *Light is the Theme,* 43.
9. Loud, *The Art Museums of Louis I. Kahn,* 151.
10. Prown, *The Architecture of the Yale Center for British Art,* 15.
11. Marshall D. Meyers, quoted in Bellinelli, *The Construction of the Kimbell Art Museum,* 23.
12. Prown, *The Architecture of the Yale Center for British Art,* 9.
13. Jules Prown, interview with the author, April 4, 2005.

14. Prown, *The Architecture of the Yale Center for British Art,* 18.
15. Sarah David, "British Art in Context at the YCBA," unpublished student paper, April 2003, author's collection.
16. Quoted in Prown, *The Architecture of the Yale Center for British Art,* 45.
17. Abba Tor, interview with the author, October 25, 2005.

EIGHT | An Architecture of Aspiration

1. Quoted in Susan Braudy, "The Architectural Metaphysic of Louis Kahn," *New York Times Magazine,* November 15, 1970, 86.
2. See Solomon, *Louis I. Kahn's Jewish Architecture,* 69.
3. Jean France, interview with the author, August 3, 2004.
4. Quoted in Jean France, "Louis Kahn and the First Unitarian Church of Rochester, New York: A Client's-Eye View," unpublished memoir, undated, author's collection.
5. Solomon, *Louis I. Kahn's Jewish Architecture,* 3.
6. Balkrishna Doshi, *Canvas of Modern Masters* (Ahmedabad, India: Vastu-Shilpa Foundation, 2000), 13.
7. Doshi, interview with the author, December 20, 2004.
8. Anant Raje, interview with the author, December 21, 2004.
9. Doshi, interview with the author, December 20, 2004
10. Balkrisha Doshi, quoted in Doshi, *Le Corbusier and Louis I. Kahn: The Acrobat and the Yogi of Architecture* (Ahmedabad, India: Vastu-Shilpa Foundation, 1992), 13.
11. Louis Kahn to William Walton, April 1, 1964, Kahn Archives.
12. Shamsul Wares, interview with the author, December 16, 2004.
13. Sue Ann Kahn, quoted in Hillyer and Pollara, *Coming to Light,* 44.
14. Memo from William Walton to The Urban Development Corporation, December 21, 1972, courtesy William vanden Heuvel.
15. Gina Pollara, interview with the author, April 2, 2013.
16. William vanden Heuvel, interview with the author, December 20, 2017.
17. Michael Kimmelman, "Decades Later, a Vision Survives," *New York Times,* September 12, 2012.

BIBLIOGRAPHY

Alofsin, Anthony. *The Struggle for Modernism: Architecture, Landscape Architecture, and City Planning at Harvard.* New York: W. W. Norton, 2002.

Bellinelli, Luca. *Louis I. Kahn: The Construction of the Kimbell Art Museum.* Milan, Italy: Skira, 1999.

Brownlee, David B., and David G. De Long. *Louis I. Kahn: In the Realm of Architecture.* New York: Rizzoli, 1991.

Dagit, Charles E., Jr. *Louis I. Kahn, Architect: Remembering the Man and Those Who Surrounded Him.* New Brunswick, N.J.: Transaction Publishers, 2013.

Fuller, R. Buckminster. *Nine Chains to the Moon.* Garden City, N.Y.: Doubleday, 1971.

Gast, Klaus-Peter. *Louis I. Kahn: The Idea of Order.* Basel and Boston: Birkhäuser Verlag, 2001.

Gilbert, Edwin. *Native Stone.* Garden City, N.Y.: Doubleday, 1956.

Goldhagen, Sarah Williams. *Louis Kahn's Situated Modernism.* New Haven, Conn.: Yale University Press, 2001.

Hillyer, Steven, and Gina Pollara. *Coming to Light: The Louis I. Kahn Monument to Franklin D. Roosevelt for New York City.* New York: The Cooper Union, 2005.

Hochstim, Jan. *The Paintings and Sketches of Louis I. Kahn.* New York: Rizzoli, 1991.

Johnson, Nell E., comp. *Light Is the Theme: Louis I. Kahn and the Kimbell Art Museum.* Fort Worth, Tex.: Kimbell Art Foundation, 1975.

Jordy, William H. *American Buildings and Their Architects.* Volumes 3–4. Garden City, N.Y.: Anchor Press/Doubleday, 1976.

Kahn, Louis. *Louis I. Kahn: Writings, Lectures, Interviews.* Edited by Alessandra Latour. New York: Rizzoli, 1991.

———. *Louis Kahn: Essential Texts.* Edited by Robert Twombley. New York: W. W. Norton, 2003.

———. *Louis Kahn to Anne Tyng: The Rome Letters 1953–1954.* Edited with commentary by Anne Griswold Tyng. New York, Rizzoli, 1997.

———. *What Will Be Has Always Been: The Words of Louis I. Kahn.* Edited by Richard Saul Wurman. New York: Rizzoli, 1986.

Khan, Nurur Rahman. *In Celebration of the Birth Centennial of Louis I. Kahn.* Dhaka, Bangladesh: University of Asia Pacific, 2001.

Komendant, August E. *18 Years with Architect Louis I. Kahn.* Englewood, N.J.: Aloray, 1975.

Kries, Mateo et al. *Louis Kahn: The Power of Architecture.* Weil am Rhein, Germany: Vitra Design Museum, 2013.

Larson, Kent. *Louis I. Kahn: Unbuilt Masterworks.* New York: Monacelli Press, 2000.

Leslie, Thomas. *Louis I. Kahn: Building Art, Building Science.* New York: George Braziller, 2005.

Lesser, Wendy. *You Say to Brick: The Life of Louis Kahn.* New York: Farrar, Straus and Giroux, 2017.

Lobell, John. *Between Silence and Light.* Boston. Mass.: Shambala, 1979.

Loud, Patricia Cummings. *The Art Museums of Louis I. Kahn.* Durham, N.C., and London: Duke University Press, 1989.

———. *History of the Kimbell Art Museum.* Fort Worth, Tex.: Kimbell Art Museum, 1987.

Marcus, George H., and William Whitaker. *The Houses of Louis Kahn.* New Haven, Conn.: Yale University Press, 2013.

Matheson, Susan B. *The Architecture of the Yale University Art Gallery.* New Haven, Conn.: Yale University Art Gallery, 2000.

McCarter, Robert. *Louis I. Kahn.* London: Phaidon, 2005.

Miller, Frederic, Morris J. Vogel, and Allen F. Davis. *Still Philadelphia: A Photographic History, 1890–1940.* Philadelphia, Pa.: Temple University Press, 1983.

Newhouse, Victoria. *Towards a New Art Museum.* New York: Monacelli, 1998.

Oliver, Richard, ed. *The Making of an Architect, 1881–1981: Columbia University in the City of New York.* New York: Rizzoli, 1981.

Papademetriou, Peter. Introduction to *Louis I. Kahn, Conversations with Students.* Edited by Dung Ngo. Houston, Tex.: Architecture at Rice Publications and New York: Princeton Architectural Press, 1998.

Prown, Jules David. *The Architecture of the Yale Center for British Art.* New Haven, Conn.: Yale Center for British Art, 2009.

Prown, Jules David, and Karen E. Denavit, eds. *Louis I. Kahn in Conversation:*

Interviews with John W. Cook and Heinrich Klotz, 1969–70. New Haven, Conn.: Yale Center for British Art, 2014.
Rykwert, Joseph. *Louis Kahn.* New York: Harry N. Abrams, 2001.
Scully, Vincent, Jr. *Louis I. Kahn.* New York: G. Braziller, 1962.
Serraino, Pierluigi. *The Creative Architect: Inside the Great Midcentury Personality Study.* New York: Monacelli Press, 2016.
Solomon, Susan G. *Louis I. Kahn's Jewish Architecture: Mikveh Israel and the Midcentury American Synagogue.* Hanover, N.H.: University Press of New England, 2009.
———. *Louis I. Kahn's Trenton Jewish Community Center.* New York: Princeton Architectural Press, 2000.
Steele, James. *Salk Institute: Louis I. Kahn.* London: Phaidon Press, 2002.
Stern, Robert A. M. *George Howe: Toward a Modern American Architecture.* New Haven, Conn.: Yale University Press, 1975.
Stern, Robert A. M., and Jimmy Stamp. *Pedagogy and Place: 100 Years of Architecture Education at Yale.* New Haven, Conn.: Yale University Press, 2016.
Strong, Ann L., and George E. Thomas. *The Book of the School: 100 Years, the Graduate School of Fine Arts of the University of Pennsylvania.* Philadelphia: Graduate School of Fine Arts, University of Pennsylvania, 1990.
Tigerman, Stanley. *Schlepping Through Ambivalence: Essays on an American Architectural Condition.* Edited by Emmanuel Petit. New Haven, Conn.: Yale University Press, 2011.
Tyng, Alexandra. *Beginnings: Louis I. Kahn's Philosophy of Architecture.* New York: Wiley, 1984.
Weiss, Paul. *The World of Art.* Carbondale: Southern Illinois University Press, 1961.
Williamson, James F. *Kahn at Penn: Transformative Teacher of Architecture.* London and New York: Routledge, 2015.
Wiseman, Carter. *I. M. Pei: A Profile in American Architecture.* New York: Harry N. Abrams, 2001.
———. *Louis I. Kahn: Beyond Time and Style.* New York: W. W. Norton, 2007.
———. *Twentieth-Century American Architecture: The Buildings and Their Makers.* New York: W. W. Norton, 2000.

INDEX

Page numbers in *italics* indicate illustrations, and *CP* followed by a number denotes a plate in the color gallery following page 86. Buildings designed by Kahn are designated by his name in parentheses.